I0422621

Career Circle

Ideas to Design Your HR Career

Jodi Brandstetter

Copyright © 2024 by Jodi Brandstetter

All Rights Reserved. Apart from any fair dealing for the purposes of research or private study, or criticism or review, as permitted under the Copyright, Designs and Patents Act 1988, this publication may only be reproduced, stored or transmitted, in any form or by any means, with the prior permission in writing of the copyright owner, or in the case of the reprographic reproduction in accordance with the terms of licenses issued by the Copyright Licensing Agency. Enquiries concerning reproduction outside those terms should be sent to the publisher.

This book is dedicated to my daughter, Lena Marcella. Your name may be from our family history, but you are our future. What I do is for you. I love you back!

Contents

Introduction   1

Part 1: Search   5

1. Career Strategy   7

2. Job Search Strategy   17

3. Build Your Brand   27

4. Think Like A Recruiter   37

5. Selection Process Strategy   45

Part 2: Integration   55

6. Prepare to Start   57

7. Your First Week   63

8. Your First 90 Days   67

9. Become A HR Business SME   71

Part 3: Advancement   77

10. Best Path   79

11. Obvious Choice   87

12. Performance Review   91

13. Relationship Building   95

Part 4: Independence   99

14. Side Hustle   101

15. Solopreneur   109

16. Entreprenuer   115

17. Coaching vs. Consulting   119

Conclusion   125

Endnotes   127

Career Circle Workbook   129

Acknowledgments   131

About Author   133

Also By   135

Introduction

Wouldn't it be wonderful if there were a guide to help craft a well-defined career strategy, ensuring that each step brings me closer to my ultimate goal?

This is a question I've pondered, and I'm not alone. The idea that we all have a clear career path from a young age rarely holds true. Many of us had no idea of what our future careers might entail during our younger years, be it in elementary, junior high, high school, or even college. In fact, I'm now 44 years old, and there are still days when I find myself uncertain about what I want to become 'when I grow up.'

What has always remained clear are my core values and unique talents. From a young age, I recognized that my life's purpose would involve serving others; I simply hadn't yet figured out the specific path I would take to fulfill that calling. Once I recognized that Human Resources (HR) was my chosen path, I sought to transform it into a fulfilling career. I also had lots of questions about my career purpose and goals.

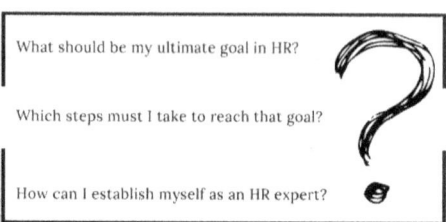

What should be my ultimate goal in HR?

Which steps must I take to reach that goal?

How can I establish myself as an HR expert?

These are common questions that all of us consider throughout our careers. A comprehensive guide offering insights into career strategy, goal setting, and actionable steps can significantly streamline the journey toward achieving our ultimate career objectives. This is precisely what I have developed with *Career Circle*.

Career Circle is a guide that provides tips and best practices on creating a career strategy, goal setting and actionable steps in each major area of your career. There are 4 major areas of a career. They include:

- **Search**

Obtaining your first job in Human Resources is the first step. Creating a career strategy with a career path will help you build the career you need. Understanding the hiring process and creating a personal brand to highlight you for the role is critical to getting the job.

- **Integration**

Being prepared for the new role, creating a solid foundation as an expert, and building key relationships will ensure that you integrate into the new position and get you closer to the next step on your career path.

- **Advancement**

Advancement is needed if you want to go up the career ladder and become a leader in HR. How can you make yourself the obvious choice for the promotion? Advancement is also obtaining the right experience and knowledge for the next step in your career.

- **Independence**

Going out on your own and building your own career or company can give you the ability to meet your career strategy yourself. Understanding the different ways to go out on your own can help you determine if being your own boss makes sense for you.

Having a guide to help you define your career strategy will help you focus on your career goals and also help build our industry up. Human Resources as an industry has a bad rep. To keep

HR relevant in the future of work, HR professionals must master their HR skills and business skills. **Career Circle** will give you a path to do just that.

Part 1: Search

S earch refers to the period during which you concentrate on defining your career strategy including career path and brand and identifying suitable opportunities to achieve your ultimate career goal.

Chapter 1

Career Strategy

M y career strategy has changed throughout my journey. When I began college, I aimed to work on Wall Street, but eventually realized that it was not the right fit for me. During an internship, I discovered Human Resources and decided to pursue it as my career. However, at that time, I had no clear idea about my HR career path, except that I wanted to work with people and enjoyed my internship experience.

About five years into my HR career, I realized that recruiting and talent acquisition were my areas of interest. So, I started learning everything related to recruiting, the industries, and the departments I recruited for. Eventually, I became the Director of Talent Acquisition for a Fortune 500 company and was on the verge of becoming the highest-ranking talent acquisition professional in the organization. But, I left the job as I realized that my path lay elsewhere. I wanted to be an entrepreneur and help multiple companies instead of just one. My career strategy changed once again, and I aspired to become a successful entrepreneur.

I believe that a career strategy changes throughout one's life, as people evolve, and develop new interests, passions, and desires for their careers. Having a tool to help you identify your career strategy throughout your life is crucial to evolving and growing confidently.

A Career Strategy includes identifying your career goals and path, creating SMART goals to achieve your career goals, and developing a plan of action. Let's explore the steps.

Self-reflection and Assessment

The first step in identifying your career goals is to reflect on your values, interests, passions, strengths, and weaknesses. Assess your current skills and knowledge to determine the direction of your career strategy.

Values are the beliefs that motivate your behavior. There are hundreds of possible values that you can list for yourself. When considering your Career Goal Values, think about the values you desire from your company, your manager, your peers, and yourself. Select 3-5 values and define them according to your understanding.

What do you enjoy doing? By answering this question, you can identify your interests. Take a few minutes to brainstorm everything that you enjoy doing, whether at work, with family and friends, or your hobbies. Your career can include your interests or hobbies, so be open to exploring all of your interests.

In the book, The Big Leap: Conquer Your Hidden Fear and Take Life to the Next Level by Gay Hendricks discusses the Zone of

Genius. This is where expertise and passion join forces. Personal satisfaction and energy live in the zone of genius.[1] What are your passions? By understanding your passion(s), you can connect them with your expertise and knowledge to create your career path.

The hardest part of self-reflection is understanding strengths and weaknesses. Strengths and weaknesses can be expertise, experience, education, skills, etc. To understand your strengths and weaknesses, you want to ask peers, leaders, family, and friends. Look at past performance reviews. Write 3-5 strengths and weaknesses.

There are several career assessments that you can take if you need more guidance. Here are a few free or low-cost assessments to consider:

- Truitiy – The Typefinder® for Career Planning[2]

- 123 test – Career Aptitude Test[3]

- My Next Move – O*Net® Interest Profiler[4]

Research

After completing your self-reflection, the next step is to do some research, which should include position, job market, and company research. There are several career paths in HR, including traditional, specialty, and technical.

Traditional

The traditional career path in Human Resources involves moving up from an individual contributor to a manager and leader. The most common entry-level roles for HR include HR Intern, HR Assistant, HR Coordinator, and HR Specialist. The most common mid-level roles are HR Generalist, HR Supervisor, HR Business Partner, and HR Manager. The most common senior-level roles are HR Director, Vice President of HR, and Chief HR Officer. In this path, knowing various HR areas is essential. The traditional career path is suitable for small to mid-size companies with a lean HR department.

Specialty

The specialty career path involves becoming an expert in one or more HR areas, such as:

- HR Strategy: Culture, Organization Design, Change Management and Analytics

- Employee Engagement: Planning, Strategy and Analytics

- Total Compensation: Benefits, Compensation, and Recognition

- Performance Management: Coaching, Goal Setting and Performance Reviews

- Talent Management: Workforce Planning, Assessment, and Succession Planning

- Talent Acquisition: Sourcing, Recruiting, Recruitment Marketing and Internal Mobility

- Learning & Development: Onboarding, Employee Development and Leadership Development

- HR Operations and Infrastructure: Structure, Policies, Compliance, Employee Relations, Technology and Budget

HR Strategy
Employee Engagement
Total Compensation
Performance Management
Talent Management
Talent Acquisition
Learning & Development
HR Operations

Becoming an expert in one area can lead to opportunities in large corporations and consulting.

Technical

The technical career path in HR involves becoming a Super User, System Administrator, or HR Architect, among others. A technical career path can include roles such as HR Helpdesk, HRIS Analyst, HR Project Manager, Data Scientist, and HRIS Architect. Technology and HR go hand in hand, and there are several types of HR Technology, such as HR Information Systems (HRIS), Payroll, Recruiting, Employee Experience, Compensation Management, Learning Management Systems (LMS), Time & Attendance, Onboarding, and Benefits Software.

In 2020, the Cognizant Center for Future of Work and Future Workplace identified 60 new HR jobs that will emerge in the future. All the roles have some level of using innovative technology, and some of them have brand-new responsibilities. The five core themes across all roles are individual and organization resilience, organization trust and safety, creativity and innovation, data literacy, and human-machine partnerships. [5]

- Individual and organization resilience – the future of HR will include a holistic approach to employee wellbeing. Examples of positions are Director of Wellbeing and Work From Home Facilitator.

- Organization trust and safety – with AI and data privacy concerns, HR will need to work with the business to mitigate bias. Examples of positions are Human Bias Officer and Strategic HR Business Continuity Director.

- Creativity and innovation – companies have gone through rapid change with the future of work and HR must create the future of work strategy. Examples of positions are The Future of Work Leader and Virtual Reality (VR) Immersion Counselor.

- Data literacy – the future of HR needs a focus on building analytics around people operations. An example of a position is HR Data Detective.

- Human-machine partnerships – robots cannot take our jobs because they cannot assess well. Companies need roles like Human-Machine Teaming Manager to help utilize the data from machines with human knowledge of the role.[6]

To learn more about your HR capabilities, use AIHR's HR 2025 Competency Assessment.[7]

Once you have an idea of the career path, the next step is to research the job market and companies. Job market research enables you to understand if the role is available, the type of companies that have the role, salary expectations, and the required skills and experience. After identifying the companies that have the role, you can conduct a deep dive review of the company.

Use sites such as Indeed.com, LinkedIn.com, and Google.com to search for roles, salaries, and company reviews. Salary.com is an excellent source of salary information. You can also ask ChatGPT questions to gain information about the job market and companies. HR is continually changing, and if you want a career in HR, you need to be prepared to learn and adapt.

SMART Goals

Now that you have an idea of the roles you want to pursue in your career, it's time to set goals to achieve success in your chosen career path. One effective approach to goal setting is using the SMART goals framework.

SMART goals are specific, measurable, achievable, relevant, and time-bound. By setting SMART goals, you can create a clear plan of action that will help you reach your career objectives.

Select a goal and work through the SMART goals steps.

Specific – Define your goal as clearly and specifically as possible. What exactly do you want to achieve?

Measurable – Determine how you will measure progress towards your goal. What metrics will you use to track your progress?

Attainable – Make sure your goal is realistic and achievable. Do you have the necessary resources, skills, and support to achieve your goal?

Realistic – Ensure that your goal is relevant to your overall career objectives. How does it fit into your larger career plan?

Time Bound – Set a deadline for achieving your goal. When do you want to have accomplished it?

SMART goals ensure that you know exactly what you need to do to accomplish the goal and the hurdles you may face to achieve the goal.

Remember to regularly review your progress towards your SMART goals and adjust them as needed. By following this framework, you can stay on track and achieve success in your chosen career path.

I have created a SMART Goals template which is included in the *Career Circle Workbook.*

Develop a Plan

Creating a plan of action is an essential step in achieving your SMART Goals. Begin by selecting one or two goals that will help you progress toward the next step of your career path. Once you have accomplished these goals, move on to the next one or two. The timeframe for achieving your goals will depend on the amount of time, energy, and effort required.

Start by developing a 90-day plan for your goals. For each SMART Goal, identify one to three areas of focus that you need to work on. Then, break down each focus area into specific tasks and set a timeline for completing them. This will help you stay focused and on track towards achieving your goals.

I have created a 90-day Plan template which is included in the *Career Circle Workbook.*

Review and Update

Your Career Strategy should never be static. You should review it annually, or more frequently if needed because the skills and tasks required for a role can change. You may have to upgrade your skills or learn new ones to remain relevant in your chosen field, and your Career Strategy can help you with this.

Just like me, your Career Strategy may evolve throughout your life, so stay open to changes. If your Career Strategy changes, create a new one.

Also you need to have the vision and the conviction to make it come true. Bob Goodwin, President of Career Club says, "It's about having a vision for where you want to go and a plan to get there. Without conviction in your own mind, convincing others becomes impossible."[8]

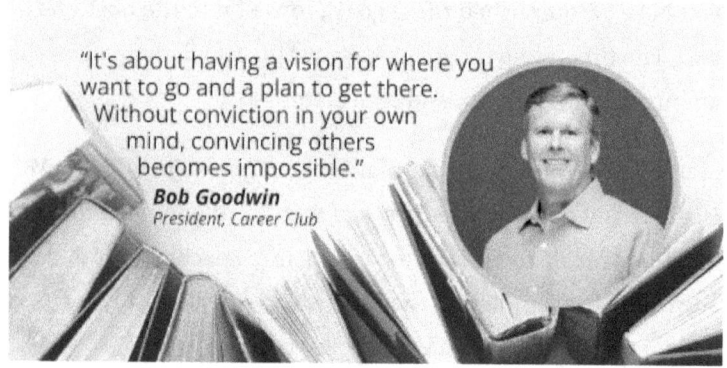

"It's about having a vision for where you want to go and a plan to get there. Without conviction in your own mind, convincing others becomes impossible."
Bob Goodwin
President, Career Club

Once you have a Career Strategy in place, you'll need a Job Search Strategy to secure the right role for your Career Strategy.

Chapter 2

Job Search Strategy

A s a recruiter by trade, I have witnessed a lot of different job search strategies. Some apply to anything and everything. Others are very particular and only apply to a few roles. And a lot get opportunities from their network, family, and friends without ever applying for a job.

Developing a comprehensive job search strategy is crucial to effectively align with your career strategy. To optimize your efforts, here are key factors to consider when formulating your strategy.

Review Your Career Strategy

Building upon the information gathered from the previous chapter, it's time to map out your next steps in advancing your career. Consider the following questions to refine your approach:

- What is the best career move today to achieve your career strategy?

- What type of company should you target for your next job in terms of industry, size, location, and culture?

- Who can you connect with to gain valuable support and assistance in your job search?

- Where can you discover potential job opportunities?

Carefully addressing these questions will help you identify suitable positions, target desirable companies, establish valuable connections, and effectively engage with potential employers.

Job Search Toolkit

Your Job Search Toolkit encompasses all the essential elements needed to position yourself as the ideal candidate for any job opportunity. These resources will support you throughout your job search. Here are the key components:

Contact Information

Establishing what contact information you want to use for your online profiles and resume, is priority number one in your job search. If a company calls, emails, or texts you and you do not respond in a timely fashion, the company will move on. If your voicemail is not set up, they will move on. If you have an inappropriate email, they will move on.

Some tips with contact information:

- Email: Create an email dedicated to your job search. This will ensure that you will see any emails that are sent. Also, always check your spam and junk folder. There is a chance an email may land in that folder from a potential employer. If it does, add the email to your contact list so that it does not go to your spam folder again.

- Phone: Call your phone number and listen to your voice-mail. If your voicemail is not set up, set it up with a professional voicemail message. Most companies will ask if you want to receive text messages. If you prefer text messages, make sure that you say yes so that the company can send texts to you.

- Address: It is up to you if you want to add your address to your resume. If you prefer not to add your address, you could add the city and state or leave it off. If you are relocating, I would suggest obtaining a PO Box in the new city. This will help the potential employer see you as a local candidate.

Ensure that you are ready for communication from potential employers before you start your job search.

Big Resume

Prepare a well-crafted and up-to-date resume that highlights your skills, qualifications, work experience, successes, technology, and education. Your resume will need to be customized for each role that you apply to.

At the beginning of your job search, create your big resume. Your big resume will have all of your information. This can be several pages. I suggest adding anything and everything to the big resume. The big resume will be used to create your customized resume.

Once you have a customized resume, save it as a new document and name it "Company. Job Title. Date". You do not want to mistakenly provide the wrong resume during the interview to the hiring manager. Recruiters and hiring managers will notice if the resume is different and this could cause you to lose the role.

Cover Letter Template

Every company, recruiter, and hiring manager has an opinion on the cover letter. Should you have one or not? Will anyone read it? And the answer is maybe.

I have seen companies specifically ask for a cover letter so I encourage you to have a cover letter template that you can use when you need a cover letter. And just like the resume, you want to customize it for each company and save it under "Company. Job Title. Date".

References

Compile a list of professional references who can vouch for your skills, work ethic, and character. Include their names, contact information, and their relationship to you. Inform your references in advance and ensure they are willing to provide a positive recommendation. Also, ask your references to recommend you on LinkedIn.

Online Presence

Employers will Google you or look at social media to find you. I had a hiring manager who searched Facebook for a candidate and got super excited about the candidate. The candidate was a former professional baseball player. Well, the candidate was not a former professional baseball player. That was a different person. I had to explain this to the hiring manager and encourage him to look at the candidate's resume to see his preferred social media platform. The candidate listed his LinkedIn profile so I had the hiring manager go there to see the candidate.

I suggest you google yourself and see what comes up. Is there someone with the same name? Did you forget that you were on different websites that had old information or inappropriate information? Does nothing come up and you look like a ghost? Take the time to review your online presence, update what needs to be updated, and add what needs to be added. The next chapter will go more into this.

Portfolio

If you can provide work samples or achievements, I would encourage you to have a portfolio to showcase these. The portfolio
can be a virtual or a physical portfolio.

Professional Attire

People always say "Dress for the job you want." Your first impression during your job search in person is typically the interview.
And what you wear does count towards that first impression.
When interviewing for an HR or leader role, you want to dress
to impress professionally. Also, you want to wear something
that you are comfortable with. Always have a professional outfit
ready to go that you feel confident and comfortable in.

Job Search Tracker

I was working on a hard-to-fill sales role for a client and finally
had a candidate who applied to the role that looked like a good
fit. My process at the time was to send my calendar for the individual to set up a time for a phone interview. And the candidate's
scheduled time on my calendar. I was excited to finally have a
potential candidate for this role. I believe in celebrating small
wins through the recruiting process! On the day of the phone
interview, I called the candidate. And he picked up (another success!)! When I introduced myself to him, he said, "I'm sorry. I
do not remember what role or company this is. Can you tell me

please?" Ouch! He did not remember the company and role that he applied to. This is one of my biggest pet peeves.

A job search tracker can help you ensure that you do not do the same thing as this candidate. Keep a record of the jobs you have applied for, including the company name, position title, application date, resume/cover letter you sent, and any relevant notes or follow-ups. This will help you stay organized and manage your job search effectively.

Now that you have your Job Search Toolkit, it is time to decide where you are going to look for job opportunities.

Job Search Logistics

When searching for jobs in the HR or leadership area, there are several websites, your network, and networking groups you can consider.

Websites

Here are some of the best websites commonly used for finding HR & Leadership job opportunities:

LinkedIn: LinkedIn is one of the top career sites and a lot of recruiters use this site to source candidates for HR and Leadership roles.

Indeed: Indeed is a leading job search engine that aggregates job postings from various sources, including company websites, job boards, and recruitment agencies. It has a user-friendly interface and allows you to filter your search based on location, salary, experience level, and more.

SHRM (Society for Human Resource Management) Job Board: The SHRM job board is specifically dedicated to HR professionals. It features job listings from reputable organizations and allows you to search by job title, location, industry, and experience level. Local SHRM associations typically have job boards as well.

HRJobs: HRJobs is a specialized job board focused on HR positions. It offers a comprehensive selection of HR job listings, including roles like HR manager, recruiter, benefits specialist, and more.

ExecuNet: ExecuNet is a specialized platform catering to executive-level job seekers. It provides access to exclusive executive job listings and offers networking opportunities with other executives and recruiters.

TheLadders: TheLadders focuses on high-level positions, including executive and senior leadership roles. It offers curated job listings and personalized job matching based on your preferences and qualifications.

Remember to consider niche or locally-focused job sites as well. However, relying solely on websites for job opportunities is not recommended.

Your Network

Employee referrals account for 30-50% of all hires according to ZIPPIA.[9]

Your networking including peers, former co-workers, family, and friends can help you get your next job. It is important to connect the dots between job opportunities and who you know.

Back in 2011, I was ready to leave the staffing company that I was working at to go back into corporate. During a happy hour with former co-workers, I let them know that I was looking for a new role. One of my former co-workers told me about an opportunity at my former employer. My former co-worker referred me to the role and I was able to get an interview and an offer. By announcing my decision to look for a new role and connecting with former co-workers, I was able to find the next job that eventually helped me achieve my career strategy.

Be open to letting the people around you know that you are looking for a new job. They know you and will be a great help to your job search.

Networking Groups

Joining networking groups is a great way to find out about potential job opportunities. There are networking groups that are focused on industry, location, and interest.

There are several HR and Talent networking groups/associations like SHRM, Association of Talent Acquisition Professionals

(ATAP), Association Training & Development (ATD), etc. Also, there are several leadership/executive networking groups like Vistage, COO Forum, The CEO Roundtable, Women Presidents' Organization, etc.

I would recommend you review or possibly attend several groups/associations before deciding on where you want to spend your money and time.

Now that you have identified the roles and companies you are targeting, understood the essential tools for your Job Search Toolkit, and considered the logistics of your search, it's time to focus on developing your personal brand and positioning yourself as the obvious choice for the role.

Chapter 3

Build Your Brand

M any professionals prioritize their personal brand solely when actively seeking a new career opportunity. While many equate their resume and LinkedIn profile with their personal brand, it's crucial to understand that these external resources showcase your personal brand rather than constituting the brand itself. To establish a compelling personal brand, it's essential to reference your Career Strategy outlined in Chapter 1. Your personal brand should feature your values, goals, strengths, knowledge, and expertise. Once you have this information, you can build resources highlighting your expertise like your resume and LinkedIn profile.

Create a Strong Personal Brand

Building a strong personal brand can significantly enhance your career search and open doors to new opportunities. Here are some steps to help you build your personal brand.

Define your professional identity:

Start by defining your professional identity, which includes understanding your values, strengths, passions, and unique selling points. Consider what sets you apart from others in your field and what you want to be known for. Look at past performance reviews or any kudos that you have received in your career. Create a working document to add all this information and continue to add information here throughout your career.

Develop a personal brand statement:

Craft a concise and compelling personal brand statement that communicates who you are, what you do, and the value you bring. This statement should be clear, memorable, and align with your career goals. For example, "I am a versatile HR professional with a passion for talent acquisition, fostering inclusive workplaces, and driving employee engagement."

Your personal brand statement will change throughout your career. Take time every year to review your statement and determine if it still works or if you need to create a new one.

Audit your online presence:

Take a comprehensive approach to evaluating your online presence by Googling your name and reviewing platforms, such as social media sites and personal websites. The key is to establish a cohesive and harmonious messaging strategy that resonates with your brand. Elevate your profiles by incorporating up-to-date and pertinent information, and don't underestimate the power of professional headshots to make a strong first impression.

Moreover, it's essential to be discerning and vigilant. Identify and eliminate any content that doesn't align with your carefully crafted personal brand or could potentially pose a hurdle in your job search journey. By curating your online presence, you can ensure that your digital footprint showcases the best and most relevant facets of your professional identity, further enhancing your career prospects.

Revamp your Resume

"A resume's purpose is not to get them a job," stated Nelly Grinfeld, a Certified Professional Resume Writer and Career Search Expert. "The resume's purpose is to get an interview so that the candidate has an opportunity to talk more in-depth about themselves."[10]

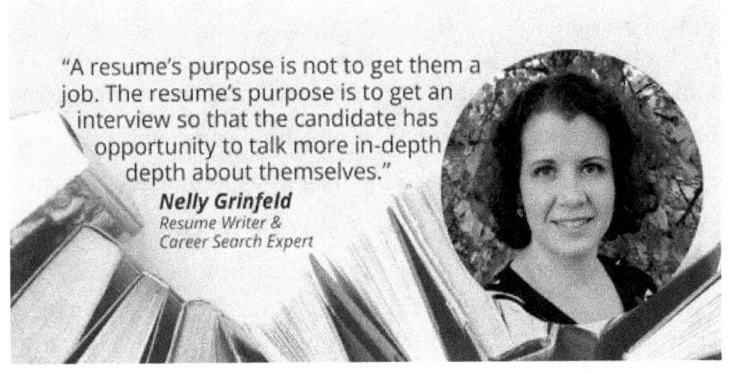

"A resume's purpose is not to get them a job. The resume's purpose is to get an interview so that the candidate has opportunity to talk more in-depth depth about themselves."

Nelly Grinfeld
Resume Writer &
Career Search Expert

Your resume serves as a marketing tool, designed to secure that all-important first interview with a company. It must effectively position you as the ideal candidate for the role. This involves creating a comprehensive resume that encompasses all your professional details, including work experience, skills, technological proficiencies, accolades, education, and more.

This comprehensive resume acts as a foundation that you should consistently update throughout your career journey. When it's time to submit your resume to a specific company, take this comprehensive document and tailor it to align with the requirements of the role you're pursuing. If you encounter challenges in crafting a compelling resume, don't hesitate to seek the assistance of a professional resume writer. Their expertise can greatly enhance your chances of standing out in a competitive job market.

Enhance your LinkedIn profile:

When interviewing Nelly Grinfeld, she spoke about the importance of having a LinkedIn profile and an online presence during the career search.[11]

LinkedIn is a powerful platform for building your professional brand. Optimize your profile by writing a compelling summary, highlighting your achievements and experiences, and using relevant keywords. Request recommendations from colleagues, supervisors, or clients to enhance your credibility.

Your LinkedIn profile should not be a copy of your resume. It should be an extension to your resume. Peg Stookey, an Executive Leadership Coach, says "Your LinkedIn is not your resume; it's your platform to tell your story on your terms."[12]

"Your LinkedIn is not your resume; it's your platform to tell your story on your terms."

Peg Stookey
Executive Leadership Coach

Curate and share content:

Elevate your professional status as a thought leader in your field by actively curating and disseminating valuable content related to HR or your specific area of expertise. Consider generating original content through blog posts or articles, contributing to industry publications, and sharing insights on social media platforms. This strategy not only solidifies your authority but also expands your visibility within your professional network and with potential employers.

While content creation may seem time-consuming, there are efficient ways to maximize your efforts. My tip is to repurpose your content in various formats. For instance, if you've written a blog post on your personal website, you can employ the following strategies:

- LinkedIn: Share a condensed version of your blog in a

LinkedIn post, repurpose the content into a more extensive LinkedIn article, and distribute it to your LinkedIn network.

- Medium.com: Did you know that you can establish a free profile on Medium.com to publish your written work? Repurpose your blog content into an article on Mediu m.com to tap into a broader readership.

- YouTube: Transform your blog content into video format. This could involve creating a YouTube short or a traditional-length video. Be sure to include a link to your original blog in the video description to guide your audience to further insights.

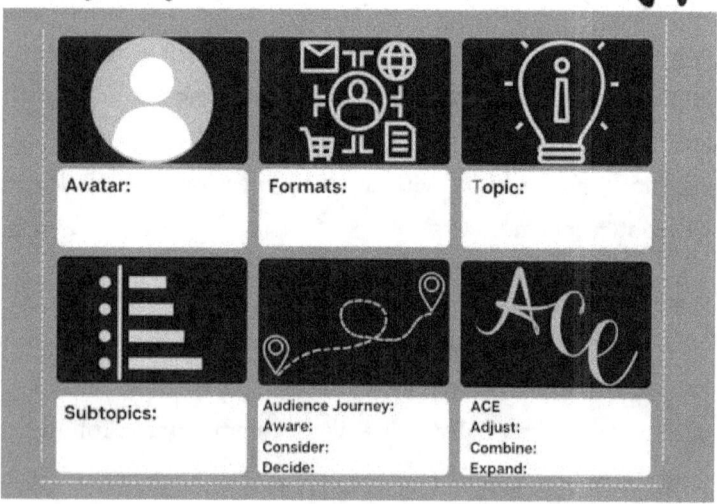

By adopting this content repurposing approach, you can efficiently leverage your valuable content across multiple platforms, optimizing your reach and influence in your professional sphere.

Network strategically:

Actively engage in professional networking both online and offline. Attend industry events, join relevant groups, participate in discussions, and connect with professionals in your field. Share your expertise, provide insights, and seek opportunities to collaborate or contribute to industry initiatives.

Numerous networking opportunities abound within the HR community. Be sure to explore the offerings on SHRM.org, which features both national and local networking options. Additionally, broaden your horizons by considering participation in networking events beyond the HR sphere. This could involve aligning with your specific industry or exploring non-profit organizations whose causes resonate with you. The key takeaway is to avoid confining your networking efforts solely to HR; diversify your connections and open doors to a wider professional landscape.

Establish a professional website or portfolio:

Consider creating a personal website or portfolio to showcase your work, projects, and accomplishments. This platform can serve as a centralized hub for potential employers or clients to learn more about you and your expertise. A noteworthy tip is to use your name for the website's URL, ensuring a professional and recognizable web address. You can purchase URLs at GoDaddy. com.

To craft your website, I recommend using Canva.com. This user-friendly low-cost platform allows you to design and customize your website, offering the added benefit of connecting it to your chosen URL. Canva's pre-made templates can streamline the design process, sparing you from starting entirely from scratch. This makes creating an impressive personal website a manageable and efficient task, ultimately bolstering your online presence and professional image.

Cultivate a strong online presence:

Consistently engage with your online community by commenting on relevant posts, participating in discussions, and sharing valuable insights. Expand your online connections by actively seeking and connecting with professionals who share your interests or work in complementary areas. Maintain a consistent presence. Regular interactions and contributions show your dedication and genuine interest in your field, which can significantly enhance your online reputation. This helps build relationships, increases your visibility, and positions you as a knowledgeable professional.

Seek speaking engagements:

Opportunities to speak at conferences and within professional organizations are abundant, particularly for HR professionals, whether on a national or local scale. Organizations like Toastmasters also offer excellent platforms for refining your public speaking skills. To secure speaking engagements, reach out to your professional network to learn from their experiences and strategies. Additionally, attending industry events is beneficial, allowing you to observe the topics and presentation styles that resonate with organizations. It's crucial to keep an eye on speaking opportunities through research, as many conferences and organizations solicit speakers. By creating a compelling speaker profile that showcases your expertise and experience, you can position yourself to secure speaking engagements that align with your knowledge, ultimately expanding your professional influence and solidifying your reputation as a respected HR professional.

Be authentic and consistent:

Your personal brand should reflect your true self. Be authentic in your interactions, communication, and content. Consistency is key—ensure that your personal brand aligns with your actions, values, and professional behavior.

Building a strong personal brand can significantly enhance your career prospects. By following these guidelines and continually refining your personal brand, you can enhance your professional presence, open doors to new opportunities, and solidify your reputation as an HR expert.

Understanding what a recruiter is looking for is the next step to obtaining your dream HR job.

Chapter 4

Think Like A Recruiter

When I chat with individuals in their career search, I always put my "Recruiter" hat on to help them see behind the curtain what a recruiter does. There is power when a candidate understands a recruiter's mind and the hiring process. Not every recruiter is the same but it is nice to get information from a recruiter when you are in a career search.

Here are my top ten tips for individuals looking for a new role:

Tip 1: Be organized with your career search.

The worst way to start a conversation with a recruiter is by asking, "What company and job is this?" This can quickly land you in the "TBNT" (Thanks, but no thanks) pile.

When I began my career search right after college, I made sure to keep a notepad with a record of all the positions I had applied for. This allowed me to be well-prepared if a recruiter or company reached out to me. With my list in hand, I could easily recall the company, the role I had applied for, the method of application, and the application date. I also diligently documented details from my conversations and any follow-ups with the company. This notepad served as my Career Search Workbook.

Fast forward to today, and technology provides us with much more efficient ways to organize our job searches. Your smartphone, for instance, is a treasure trove of information. However, the key takeaway remains the same: staying organized is crucial. Make sure you always know which companies you've applied to and be prepared for unexpected phone calls from recruiters.

Tip 2: Connect with HR, Recruiters, and industry professionals.

Networking and building connections can significantly impact your career search, potentially unlocking new opportunities. It's essential to invest time in connecting with fellow HR professionals to gain valuable insights. Connect with Recruiters to understand the job market and get advice. Additionally, establish connections with individuals working in the industry or at companies you're considering. This will help you understand their perspectives and the potential dynamics of your future workplace.

Set a goal to connect with at least one or more individuals each week. Consider scheduling a Zoom meeting, a casual coffee chat, or a lunch meeting to foster these relationships.

Tip 3: Confidence is important.

Confidence is the key to unlocking career opportunities. Your confidence is reflected in your posture, words, and even on your resume and LinkedIn profile. It's crucial to exude confidence in your professional documents. Seek feedback from people you trust and admire to help boost your self-assurance.

Before an interview, consider asking someone for a pep talk to bolster your confidence. If you prefer to work on your confidence independently, practice positive affirmations. Stand in front of a mirror and recite affirmations to yourself.

Before significant meetings or speaking engagements, I often revisit my LinkedIn recommendations. Many of my former colleagues and employees have written glowing recommendations for me. This not only elevates my self-esteem but also enables me to present a confident version of myself in any room.

Tip 4: Always be prepared.

The Boy Scouts are absolutely right about the importance of always being prepared. In your career search, being prepared can encompass several critical elements. First and foremost, it's essential to know precisely the type of company and role you are seeking. Additionally, having your resume and personal brand in order is vital, as is being ready for interviews and having a clear understanding of your expectations from a role.

Take the time to thoroughly research potential roles and companies to ensure they align with your career goals and values. Before you start applying for jobs, make sure your personal brand is well-crafted, which includes having a well-prepared resume and an optimized LinkedIn profile. Prepare for interviews by conducting mock interviews, developing a list of questions to ask the interviewer, and boosting your confidence beforehand. Clearly define your non-negotiables for a role, including factors such as the company culture, job duties, compensation, location, and benefits. This will help you narrow down your options and focus on the right opportunities for you.

By being proactive and prepared in these areas, you'll increase your chances of finding a job that truly suits your aspirations and needs.

Tip 5: Apply to multiple sites for the same job.

There's a common misconception among candidates that applying to a role on multiple platforms can be detrimental. I disagree. The organization's career site remains the preferred application channel, as recruiters regularly review their Applicant Tracking System (ATS) there. I understand that the career site isn't always the most user-friendly option.

If you find it more convenient to apply through job posting sites such as Indeed or LinkedIn, by all means, go ahead. My suggestion, though, is to also take the time to apply through the career site. The reason is that there's a possibility a recruiter may not review all resumes submitted via job posting sites. By applying through both channels, you increase your chances of having your resume reviewed by a recruiter or hiring manager.

Tip 6: Flip rejection on its head.

Rejection is an integral part of your career search. Rarely does someone secure a job with just one application. Typically, you need to apply to multiple positions before landing one. It's important to remember that even recruiters face rejection, as candidates decline conversations, interviews, and job offers, and occasionally fail to show up on their first day.

Both candidates and recruiters share the experience of rejection, and it's essential to reframe how we perceive it. Rejection brings us closer to finding the right opportunity. Each "no" paves the way for a future "yes." Receiving a rejection can provide the confidence that the role or opportunity wasn't the best fit.

One effective approach to flip the script on rejection is to embrace it. For instance, when reaching out to connect with people on LinkedIn, set a goal for the number of rejections you aim to collect. Suddenly, you'll find yourself actively seeking out rejection to achieve your goal, which takes the power away from the negative aspect of rejection.

Tip 7: Ghosting is not cool (company and candidate).

Ghosting can occur from either side of the equation. A company may cease contact with a candidate, or a candidate may disengage from a company. When communication dwindles, it can signal a loss of interest, but it can also result from a simple over-sight. My recommendation is to avoid ghosting and, if you unintentionally do so, have the willingness to reconnect and extend an apology. Everyone involved in the hiring process is human, and we are all susceptible to making mistakes.

Tip 8: Patience and Persistence are needed.

The hiring process often resembles a roller coaster ride, complete with its own set of ups and downs. At times, it can feel like you're going upside down, sideways, and even backward. Maintaining patience and persistence is key to navigating this roller coaster successfully.

Patience comes into play when dealing with the delays and long waits between different stages of the hiring process. It's crucial to remain composed and focused, even when faced with the unpredictability of the journey.

Persistence is equally vital as it empowers you to consistently reach out and follow up on opportunities. In a competitive job market, tenacity can set you apart and increase your chances of landing the job you desire

Tip 9: Know your worth.

When it comes to compensation, it's crucial to have a clear understanding of your personal needs and preferences, not only for yourself but also for your family. If you're uncertain about the appropriate compensation for a particular role, it's a good idea to visit websites like Salary.com or Indeed.com to access comprehensive salary data. Take the time to create two lists: one for 'must-have' benefits and perks, and another for 'nice-to-have' ones. Avoid making assumptions about your current salary's alignment with the market rates. Be your own advocate, and empower yourself with the knowledge needed to negotiate your compensation effectively.

Tip 10: Send a Thank You Note.

A thank-you note can significantly impact your chances of receiving a job offer. In numerous instances, when two candidates were being evaluated, the one who sent a thank-you note ended up receiving the offer. There is a common misconception that all candidates send thank-you notes, but this is not the case.

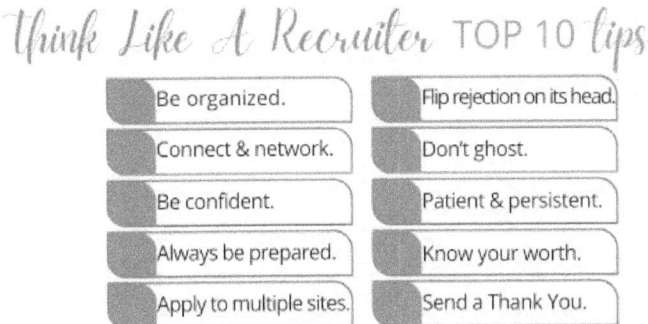

Think Like A Recruiter TOP 10 tips

- Be organized.
- Connect & network.
- Be confident.
- Always be prepared.
- Apply to multiple sites.
- Flip rejection on its head.
- Don't ghost.
- Patient & persistent.
- Know your worth.
- Send a Thank You.

I encourage you to reach out to recruiters to gain valuable insights and perspectives on your job search. Be open to taking advice from professionals who regularly review resumes and interview candidates. This can significantly enhance your chances of securing your next role.

Now that you have received guidance from a recruiter, the next step is to prepare for the selection process. There is a strategy that can help you effectively engage decision-makers and increase your chances of landing a new job.

Chapter 5

Selection Process Strategy

E very company follows a unique selection and hiring process. Typically, they do not disclose the steps until you are actively engaged in the process. Your conduct during this process can significantly impact your chances of securing the position. Being well-prepared for any scenario can increase your likelihood of receiving an offer. Moreover, having a clear understanding of your expectations in terms of the role, company, compensation, and benefits will help you secure an offer that aligns with your desires and requirements.

In my book, Hire By Design, I provided the common steps of the selection process.

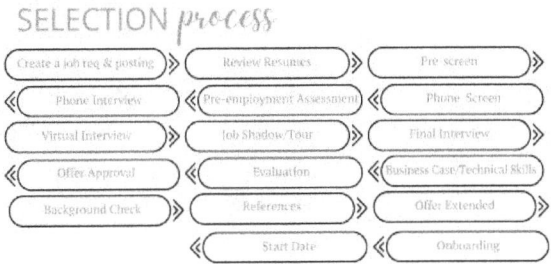

Here is a breakdown of all potential steps in the selection process and how to prepare for each.

Application:

When applying for a role, ensure that you provide all the information the company requests fully. Customize your cover letter and resume for the role you are applying to. Highlight specific achievements, experiences, and skills that are relevant to the job description. Show how you can contribute to the company's HR goals and address any specific requirements mentioned in the job posting.

If a cover letter is not mandatory, you are not obliged to submit one. The necessity of a cover letter remains a topic of debate within the HR community. In my opinion, it's best to provide a cover letter only when it is required or when it offers valuable additional information, such as explaining your willingness to relocate to the area, which can help the company better understand your interest in the role.

Pre-screen:

A pre-screen consists of questions designed to help a company assess if you meet the minimum qualifications for the role. It's crucial, as a candidate, to complete the pre-screen honestly and thoroughly. Skipping questions or leaving them incomplete can result in your application being marked as 'incomplete,' which recruiters may not review.

If you have concerns about how to answer a question, it's advisable to invest some time in researching on platforms like Glassdoor, Indeed Forums, or the company's website to determine if your response might disqualify you from the position. It's better to have this information upfront rather than invest in the application process only to be disqualified later on.

If, at any stage of the selection process, you encounter red flags or have concerns about the company or the role, remember that you have the right to withdraw from the process. Don't feel obligated to continue just because you've already begun. You are your best advocate.

Pre-employment Assessment:

The dreaded pre-employment assessment! Not many candidates look forward to these, but I've witnessed their benefits. When companies leverage these assessments effectively, they can help ensure that a candidate is not only a good fit for the role and the company but can also aid in training and development once the individual starts. In essence, it can be a win-win for both the employee and the company.

Before taking the assessment, it's crucial to understand its requirements, including the time commitment and necessary technology. Most assessments are designed for computer-based completion, often with timed sections, so ensure you're in a quiet space where you won't be interrupted and can stay focused.

An assessment is just one part of the overall selection process. Many companies use it to gain insights into a candidate and to formulate interview questions that help assess their suitability for the role.

How a company uses these assessments can offer you a glimpse into its company culture. If you believe they aren't using the assessment in the right way or if you have concerns, I recommend considering whether to continue with the process.

Interview:

An interview is your chance to showcase your expertise and prove that you are the best fit for the job. There are various types of interviews, and you may go through several rounds. Here are some tips for each type of interview.

Phone Interview:

Phone interviews are typically conducted by HR or recruiters. They serve to ensure you meet the qualifications and to get to know you better. Be well-prepared with a charged phone, earbuds, or a quiet location, and have the job posting and your resume in front of you. Remember that your voice can sound more pleasant when you smile, so keep a positive tone.

Familiarize yourself with common HR interview questions and practice your responses. Highlight your expertise in areas such as employee relations, talent acquisition, performance management, training and development, HR analytics, and compliance.

When given the opportunity to ask questions, inquire about the company, the hiring manager, and the role. You can also discuss the interview process, compensation, and benefits. Have a compensation range in mind, and be open to adjusting it based on the benefits offered.

Video Interview:

Video interviews can be one-way or two-way. In a one-way interview, you answer pre-recorded questions. For two-way interviews, be prepared with the video platform ready, use headphones, maintain eye contact, smile, and nod to show your engagement. Have the job posting and your resume nearby, and note down your questions. Ask about the next steps and thank the interviewer at the end.

Onsite Interview:

Many tips from phone and video interviews apply to onsite interviews. Ensure you know the office location, arrive 15 minutes early, and have your resume, the job posting, and your questions with you. Dress comfortably but professionally, and be mindful of strong perfumes or colognes. Turn your phone off or set it to vibrate. Avoid answering calls or texts during the interview. Ask for a business card from each person you meet.

Panel Interview:

In a panel interview, address each panel member individually, use their names when answering questions, and make eye contact with everyone. When asking questions, you can choose to ask each panel member the same or different questions. Collect business cards from each panel member for follow-up thank-yous.

Lunch/Dinner Interview:

In one of my first real jobs after college, I had to do a lunch interview. I was so nervous! How do you interview while eating? The reason my former manager included a lunch interview was to ensure that I would fit well on her team. It was more of a get-to-know-you type of interview. We did not talk a lot about the role but more about ourselves. Thankfully, I did not get any food in my teeth, my picky eating habits did not scare them and I got the job.

Lunch or dinner interviews are more relaxed and focus on getting to know you. Choose easy-to-eat foods and use proper table manners. If you have any remaining questions, this is a good time to ask, as it's often the final interview stage before an offer.

After the interview:

Always send personalized thank-you notes or emails to express your gratitude for the opportunity. This small gesture can leave a positive impression and keep you on the employer's radar.

Tour:

A company tour can provide you with a holistic view of the organization. Nowadays, some companies offer virtual tours on their websites or as part of the interview process. Any opportunity to explore the work environment can significantly contribute to making a well-informed decision.

Job Shadow:

Job shadows offer candidates a valuable glimpse into the day-to-day workings of a company. If you have the opportunity to job shadow, make the most of it. Engage with the individuals you're shadowing, inquire about their experiences, observe the work environment, and request to see the technology and tools you'd be using. This immersive experience can help you assess whether you would genuinely enjoy working there and may also spark additional questions.

If you have reservations about a role, don't hesitate to request a job shadow or spend time with potential co-workers. This first-hand exposure can assist you in making a well-informed decision.

Offer and Negotiations:

Before considering the job offer, celebrate! Receiving an offer is amazing! A company sees your talent and wants you to join the team. That is great news!

When presented with a job offer, it is essential to approach the situation with careful consideration and professionalism. To begin, resist the urge to rush into a decision and instead express your gratitude for the offer while requesting time for a thorough review. Three days to a week is an acceptable timeframe to review an offer. Take the opportunity to scrutinize the offer letter, paying close attention to key details such as salary, benefits, job responsibilities, and other terms and conditions. It's important to assess how well the offer aligns with your career goals, taking into account factors like location, work-life balance, and growth potential. If you believe there is room for improvement, approach negotiations with tact and respect.

Negotiating an employment offer is a significant step in ensuring that the terms meet your expectations. Start by researching to grasp industry standards for salaries and benefits, which will strengthen your case. When discussing your concerns or desired changes with the employer, maintain a professional and respectful tone. Emphasize your skills, experience, and the value you bring to the company during negotiations. Keep in mind that negotiations can encompass various aspects beyond just salary, such as additional benefits, flexible work arrangements, or professional development opportunities. Be prepared to provide specific reasons for your requests and remain open to compromises to find mutually beneficial solutions.

Additionally, seek clarity on any terms that may be unclear and assess whether the company's culture aligns with your values. Inquire about the next steps, such as the start date and onboarding process. If you have reservations about the contract, considering seeking legal advice is a wise precaution. Once you are content with the offer and negotiations are resolved, confirm your acceptance in writing. Finally, regardless of your decision, express your appreciation to the employer for extending the offer, as this professionalism can create a positive impression for future opportunities.

Background Check:

Background checks can vary significantly from one company to another, often depending on factors like the nature of the business, contractual requirements, or the type of work involved. These checks typically encompass various elements, such as criminal history, drug screening, credit assessment, references, employment verification, and education verification.

During the interview process, it's perfectly acceptable to inquire about the specific components included in the background check, as this demonstrates your thoroughness and a desire to understand all aspects of the hiring process. As a recruiter, I view such inquiries as responsible and not a red flag.

If you have questions or concerns about the background check, it's best to discuss them with the recruiter or the HR department, rather than the hiring manager, unless they are part of the HR team. Hiring managers may not have the necessary information, and raising such questions with them could potentially raise concerns about your candidacy.

It's important to note that not all findings in a background check will automatically disqualify you from the hiring process. What can jeopardize your candidacy is falsifying information on your application or background check form. Being truthful is crucial; I've encountered cases where candidates had items on their background checks that didn't hinder their offers but lost opportunities due to inaccuracies.

Many states now have 'ban the box' legislation, which means that companies cannot inquire about your criminal history upfront, but this question may still come up.

For employment and education verifications, ensure you provide accurate contact information for the relevant institutions. Delays can occur when waiting for these verifications, so it's in your best interest to ensure the company has all the necessary details to complete the background check smoothly.

Regarding drug screens, if you are on any medication, be ready to provide a prescription to validate your use. Also, be prepared for a urine screen. In cases where you can't produce a sample, the lab may report that you refused to comply.

I once had a challenging experience with a drug test where I couldn't provide a sample immediately. Unfortunately, I couldn't reschedule or leave and come back, so I sat for about 20 minutes drinking water to help facilitate the sample. I wish I had been better prepared, such as by hydrating before the test.

Reference checks are an opportunity for you to choose the individuals a company can contact to gain more insight into your qualifications. Ideally, you should have 3 to 5 potential references, which can include former managers, co-workers, or peers. It's essential to ensure that your references are well-informed about the company, the specific role, and any details that will help them effectively highlight your skills and work. Additionally, it's a good practice to express your gratitude with a thank-you note when your references are contacted

A background check can vary in duration, taking anywhere from a few days to a week or even longer. It's a good practice to maintain communication with the company and inquire if there are any steps you can take to expedite the process. The ultimate objective is to have the background check completed as swiftly as possible.

Onboarding:

While waiting to start your new role, you can begin announcing it, connecting with your future colleagues, and getting ready for your first day. In the next section of the book, you'll find a dedicated chapter that provides detailed guidance on preparing to start a new position.

The selection process can vary in duration from a day to several weeks. Be prepared for any challenges or opportunities that may arise during this period. Make sure you get all your questions answered and secure the offer you deserve.

Now is the time to start thinking about integrating into the new company and creating opportunities to showcase your skills for career advancement.

Part 2: Integration

I ntegration refers to the period during which you concentrate on building your career within an organization.

Chapter 6

Prepare to Start

C ongratulations on landing the job that will help your career strategy take off! With your two-week notice given and start date confirmed, you are now waiting to start your new job. So, what can you do to prepare for this new venture?

Remember that first impressions began during the selection process and will continue throughout your first week on the job. By preparing for your start date, you can maintain a positive first impression. Here are some steps you can take to prepare for your new job:

Smooth Transition

Before you start your new job, it's important to wrap up any loose ends in your current role and ensure a smooth transition for your replacement. This will help you start your new job with a clear mind. Additionally, it's a good idea to connect with your co-workers, leaders, and anyone who was a part of your time at the company. Thank them and ask them to continue to connect after you leave. Leaving on a positive note is important because you never know if your career strategy will bring you back to the company or connect you with former colleagues in the future.

In 2007, I made the tough decision to leave my role and pursue opportunities that would allow me to grow my recruitment knowledge and expertise. I loved my work and colleagues but there was no next step for me at the company. However, from 2007 to 2011, I continued to stay in touch with my former co-workers. During a happy hour, one of them told me about an opportunity at the company that would be a great fit for my career strategy. I applied, interviewed, and eventually landed the role of Talent Acquisition Consultant, which later led to roles as Manager and Director.

By leaving on a positive note and continuing to nurture my relationships with former co-workers, I was able to land the right job for my career strategy. This is a testament to the importance of maintaining positive connections in your professional network, even after you've left a role.

Announcement

Landing a new job is a big accomplishment, and it's important to celebrate with your loved ones and business network.

Here are a few ways to announce the new role:

- Post on Social Media – Share your new role on your social media accounts. In your post, include your job title, the name of the company, and what excites you about this new opportunity.

- Email – Send an email to individuals who have helped you through your career search, those in the same industry or field, and your supporters. Let them know about your new job and express your gratitude for their support.

- Have a party – A party is a great way to celebrate your accomplishment. Whether it's a happy hour, dinner, or a virtual Zoom party, it's a fun way to commemorate your achievement.

By announcing and celebrating this milestone, you will feel excited and motivated for your new role. It's important to take the time to recognize your achievement and the support of those around you.

Connections

Staying productive during the transition period is key, and connecting with key individuals is a great way to achieve that.

Before your start date, I recommend reaching out to your new colleagues and manager. This will allow you to start building relationships early on and gain a better understanding of the company culture. You can connect through a variety of methods, such as phone, email, or even social media.

By taking the initiative to reach out before your start date, you will demonstrate your enthusiasm and eagerness to be a part of the team. Additionally, it will help you to hit the ground running on your first day and show that you are ready to contribute to the company's success.

Here is an example email that you can send to your new manager.

Next start building your professional network by utilizing LinkedIn. Start connecting with individuals at your new company, influencers in your industry, and anyone else who you believe would be beneficial in your new role.

For instance, if your new role involves recruiting, connect with co-workers such as hiring managers and individuals in the departments you will be recruiting for, potential candidates, as well as other recruiters in the industry.

By actively building your LinkedIn network, you will expand your reach and open up new opportunities for learning and growth. It is also an excellent way to stay connected with colleagues and industry peers, as well as stay up-to-date on industry news and trends.

Review

To ensure a smooth transition and a successful start in your new role, review your job description and research the company's values, mission, and culture. There are several resources you can utilize to gather information such as the company's website, Glassdoor, LinkedIn, and Indeed.

Additionally, reach out to individuals at the company and ask to connect before your start date. This will not only help you to build relationships early on but also provide you with insights into the company culture and any tips they may have for a smooth start.

By taking the time to do this research and networking, you will have a better understanding of what is expected of you and how you can contribute to the company's success. This will help you to hit the ground running and be more confident in your new role.

Ready for Day One

Here are some things that you can do to prepare for your first day:

1. Get enough rest the night before: Make sure you get a good night's sleep so you can wake up feeling refreshed and alert.

2. Plan your commute or check your technology: Check the route to your new workplace and plan how long it will take you to get there. It's always a good idea to leave early on your first day to avoid any unexpected delays. Or if your role is remote, ensure that your technology is ready to go for your first day.

3. Dress appropriately: Make sure you know the dress code for your new workplace and choose your outfit accordingly.

4. Bring necessary documents: Make sure you have all the required documents such as your ID, and any other paperwork your employer may have requested.

5. Prepare questions: Be prepared to ask questions and take notes on anything you may need clarification on.

6. Be positive and open-minded: Go into your first day with a positive attitude and be open-minded to learning new things and meeting new people.

7. Define your employee brand: How do you want other employees and leaders to view you as an employee? Write down your vision of yourself in this new role and new company.

By following these steps, you'll be ready to start your new job with confidence and make a great first impression. Now it is time to make your first week a success.

Chapter 7

Your First Week

Your first impression may have begun during the hiring process, but your first week on the job can truly solidify that impression. After following all the tips to prepare for your first day, it's time to start your new job with confidence and enthusiasm. Here are some tips for your first week on the job:

When you walk through the doors or log into the system for the first time, you are building your employee brand at your new company. To build your brand positively, ensure you are on time with a positive mindset and a smile. The first day can be overwhelming with paperwork, training, and meet-and-greets. Each person you meet is beginning to see you as an employee, so make sure they see you as you wish to be seen. Thankfully, you are prepared because you wrote down your employee brand before you started. At the end of your first day, jot down some notes on how the day went and any to-dos for the next day. Your Career Circle Workbook has some prompt questions to help you with this.

With the first day nerves behind you, day two is a great opportunity to show your expertise and how you can be an asset to the team. Refer to your notes from day one and attend to any remaining to-dos on your list. This is a great time to start to observe the people around you to get a better feel for the work environment. You may want to write down some notes from your observation or any questions you may have based on your observations.

Ensure you have time on your calendar to review policies, and procedures, and understand the various types of technology you will be using. Familiarize yourself with the company's policies, procedures, and employee handbook. Pay attention to essential information like attendance, time-off policies, communication protocols, and any relevant guidelines. Familiarize yourself with the tools, software, and systems used in your role. If necessary, request training or access to these resources. Take notes or create a cheat sheet to refer to later.

Familiarize yourself with the various departments within the organization. Identify key departmental leaders, understand their roles, and locate their respective departments within the building (if applicable). Begin compiling a list of individuals you would like to meet during your tenure. Consider connecting with leaders from departments you directly support, as well as individuals who have longstanding experience with the company and new hires. Gaining diverse perspectives from within the company can provide valuable insights into your potential role and where you can make a meaningful impact.

The end of the week is a great time to seek feedback and understand what you should focus on during your second week on the job. Seek regular feedback from your supervisor and colleagues to gauge your progress and identify areas for improvement. Don't hesitate to ask questions and seek guidance when needed. It demonstrates your enthusiasm and commitment to learning.

As you wrap up your first week on the job, it's important to start preparing for the weeks ahead. Add any pending tasks or follow-ups to your calendar or to-do list to ensure they are not forgotten. Setting aside time to plan your week can help you stay organized and focused on your goals.

Next week presents a great opportunity to start building relationships within the organization. Consider scheduling coffees, lunches, or meetings with individuals you want to get to know better. This could include colleagues from different departments, senior leaders, or peers who share similar interests or roles. Building a strong network early on can help you navigate the organization more effectively and can also lead to valuable collaborations in the future.

Keep an eye out for any company events or gatherings happening next week. These events can provide additional networking opportunities and can also help you get a better sense of the company culture. Whether it's a team-building activity, a departmental meeting, or a social event, attending these gatherings can help you integrate into the organization and establish yourself as a valuable team member.

Just like the first day of school, your first day at a new job can evoke a range of emotions from excitement to nervousness. Before you walk through the front door or log into your computer, take a moment to give yourself a pep talk.

During the first week on the job, focus on making a positive impression, getting oriented, and establishing a foundation for success. Remember, it's an opportunity to build positive relationships and set the stage for your future at the company. Stay proactive, open-minded, and focused on learning and contributing to make the most of this crucial period.

As you reflect on your first week and prepare for the next phase of your journey, remember that the first 90 days are crucial for setting the tone for your tenure at the company. In the next chapter, we'll delve deeper into how you can continue to acclimate, contribute, and thrive in your new role.

Chapter 8

Your First 90 Days

T he first 90 days can be eye-opening, not just for you but also for your manager and peers. In my experience, this period has been instrumental in determining if a company and role are a good fit for me. During this time, I make it a priority to deeply understand my role, the organization, and how I can contribute effectively.

Your First 90 Days

Establish Clear Expectations
Learn About the Company's Culture & Processes
Build Relationships
Seek Feedback
Skill Development
Deliver Results & Maintain a Positive Attitude

Establish Clear Expectations

To be successful in your first 90 days on the job, it's important to take several proactive steps. Start by establishing clear expectations for your role, responsibilities, and goals. Discuss these with your manager to ensure alignment and seek clarification on any ambiguities. Understanding what is expected from you is key to a successful start.

Learn About the Company's Culture and Processes

Next, take the time to learn about the company's culture, values, and work processes. Observe how successful employees in your team operate and interact. This knowledge will help you integrate smoothly into the organization and contribute effectively. Adapting to the company's culture and values is crucial for fitting in and building credibility within the organization. Align your actions and behavior with the cultural norms while remaining true to yourself. Show respect for the company's values and demonstrate your commitment to its success.

Build Relationships

Building relationships with your colleagues, team members, and other stakeholders is crucial during the first 90 days. Take the initiative to introduce yourself, ask questions, and seek guidance from others. Attend team lunches or social events to get to know your colleagues on a personal level. Building these relationships early on can help you establish a strong support network within the organization.

Seek Feedback

Seeking feedback from your manager, co-workers, and others who work closely with you is essential for understanding your strengths and areas for improvement. Use this feedback constructively to adapt and grow in your role. Being proactive and showing initiative is also key. Identify opportunities to contribute and add value, suggest innovative ideas, and take on additional responsibilities when appropriate.

Skill Development

Skill development is important during your first 90 days. Identify areas where you can enhance your skills to excel in your role. Embrace the company's culture and values, adapting your approach to align with cultural norms while remaining authentic. Delivering on commitments, maintaining a positive attitude, and seeking mentorship are additional ways to ensure a successful start to your new role.

Deliver Results and Maintain a Positive Attitude

During your first 90 days, focus on delivering results and adding value to the organization. Be proactive in identifying opportunities to contribute and suggest innovative ideas. Maintain a positive attitude, even in the face of challenges, and demonstrate your enthusiasm for your role and the company's mission.

Remember, the first 90 days are crucial for setting the foundation of your professional journey in the organization. Use this time to learn, adapt, and establish yourself as a valuable member of the team.

Next, it is time to show that you can be a continuous learner and be called a subject matter expert in Human Resources and Business.

Chapter 9

Become A HR Business SME

H R professionals must evolve into business subject matter experts to ensure that HR remains a strategic function within an organization. They need to transcend mere familiarity with HR practices and delve into the broader business context. This necessitates a commitment to continuous learning, keeping abreast of both HR trends and broader business developments.

Staying up to date with HR trends is important to continue being a subject matter expert in HR. There are several ways to stay up to date in HR, including reading HR-focused books and articles, attending HR events such as webinars and conferences, and connecting with HR professionals. One way I ensure that I obtain up-to-date HR information is through Google Alerts (https://www.google.com/alerts). Google Alerts will update you on any keyword searches that you provide via email. The alerts can be weekly or daily. My recommendation is to include the following keywords: "Human Resources," HR, "Talent Management," "Employee Relations," Recruitment, "Diversity and Inclusion," "Performance Management," "HR Technology,"

"Workplace Culture," and "Employee Engagement." I would also recommend including your name, your company name, plus any business keywords that will help you stay up to date with HR and business.

Amy Clark, CHRO and Executive Coach says, "I always start with areas outside of HR because I believe to be effective in HR, we are business people first that happen to have expertise in HR."[13]

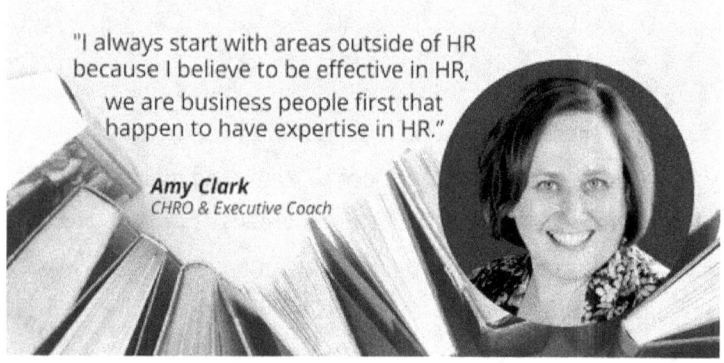

"I always start with areas outside of HR because I believe to be effective in HR, we are business people first that happen to have expertise in HR."

Amy Clark
CHRO & Executive Coach

A crucial element in achieving this expertise is cultivating a growth mindset, as emphasized by Peg Stookey in her interview. A growth mindset involves believing in one's capacity to grow and develop skills, embracing challenges, persisting in the face of setbacks, and viewing effort as a pathway to mastery.

To adopt a growth mindset, HR professionals should approach learning as a lifelong journey. They should actively pursue opportunities to expand their knowledge and skills, whether through formal education, self-directed study, or hands-on learning experiences. By doing so, HR professionals can deepen their understanding of business dynamics and make more impactful contributions to their organization's strategic goals.[14]

Before delving into understanding their organization's business, HR professionals must have a solid grasp of all business areas. While pursuing an MBA is one route to gaining this understanding, it's not the sole path. Comprehensive business comprehension can be achieved through self-study, specialized courses, workshops, and on-the-job learning. The key is a dedication to continuous education and staying informed about the latest trends and practices in the business world.

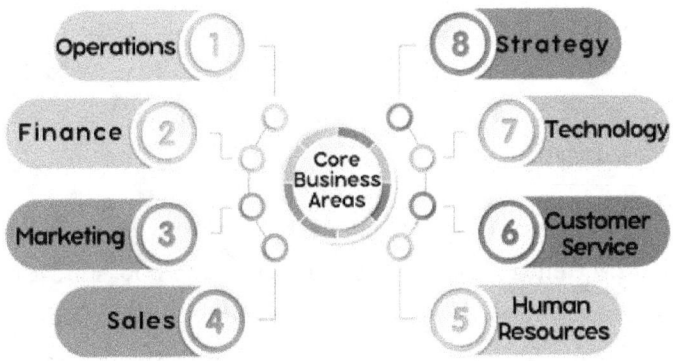

There are eight core areas in a business including Operations, Finance, Marketing, Sales, Human Resources, Customer Service, IT/Technology, and Strategy. Gaining knowledge in all these areas will help you see a holistic view of how a business works. Here are some ways to become knowledgeable in all of these areas.

Study the Business Model: Understand how your company creates, delivers, and captures value. This includes knowing the type of products and services the company creates, the target audience to sell them to, revenue streams, and key partnerships. Also, understand the company's goals and initiatives.

Learn from Co-workers and Leaders: Build relationships with co-workers and leaders from different areas of the business to gain insights into their roles and responsibilities. Selecting mentors from other areas of the business can also provide guidance and business knowledge.

Take Courses or Training: Consider taking courses or training programs in business fundamentals, such as finance, marketing, operations, and human resources. Online platforms like Coursera, Udemy, and LinkedIn Learning offer a wide range of courses. Your organization may have courses or training that you can utilize as well.

Stay Informed: There are several ways to stay up to date on industry trends. There are so many amazing books out there that are easy to read and provide you with a wealth of business knowledge. If you prefer short-form writing, consider reading articles from business sites like Forbes, Business Insider, etc. Podcasts are also a great way to gain knowledge if you are more of an auditory learner. Follow relevant blogs, news outlets, and industry publications.

Attend Conferences and Events: Consider attending events that focus on different areas of business to learn. These can include events that your company hosts like their annual sales meeting. Events also give you the ability to network and meet new people.

Gain Hands-on Experience: Try to gain experience in different areas of the business through projects or job rotations. This will give you a broader perspective and deeper understanding of how different functions interact.

Seek Feedback: Request feedback from peers, leaders, and mentors on your understanding of the core areas of business. They can help you identify the areas you need to focus on.

By following these steps, you can become a knowledgeable business professional who understands all the core areas of a business, making you a valuable asset to your organization.

Now it is time to consider your next step in your career: advancement.

Part 3: Advancement

A dvancement refers to the period during which you concentrate on defining your next step in your career strategy and identifying the best path and suitable opportunities to achieve that.

Chapter 10

Best Path

When it comes to advancing your career, choosing the appropriate role within your company is crucial. The ideal position could lie within the HR department, or it might be in another department altogether. The choice largely depends on your specific career goals and the direction you wish to pursue. It's worth noting that an internal career move can lead to various outcomes: it can be a step forward, a step back, or even a side step.

A Step Forward

A conventional approach to career advancement involves taking a step forward. This often entails moving up within your organization's hierarchy, such as ascending to a managerial position or transitioning into an executive role. If your career strategy involves acquiring additional responsibilities, pursuing such a path is generally the most effective way to achieve your goals. Typically, these advancements occur within the same department where you have established expertise and experience.

Example Career Path

The traditional career advancement path often requires a considerable amount of time to achieve, particularly in smaller companies. If the desired role is not available within your organization when you are ready to move up, you may need to explore opportunities outside of your current workplace. Additionally, it can be beneficial to consider advancement options beyond your current department. If your skills and experience align with another department's requirements, it's worthwhile to keep an eye out for potential opportunities in that area as well.

By identifying the specific promotions or roles you aspire to, you can actively work towards building your career within your current organization while staying aligned with your overall career strategy. This approach allows you to stay on track and seize the right opportunities as they arise.

A Step Back

The concept of taking a step back in your career may initially seem synonymous with a demotion, but it is not necessarily so straightforward. It can indeed involve a decrease in pay or a lower pay grade, which can be seen as a demotion in that sense. However, from a broader perspective, a step back can also present valuable opportunities for personal and professional growth.

While the title or compensation may take a hit, stepping back can offer the chance to enhance one's knowledge and experience in a new area of business. This shift can contribute to an individual's overall business acumen and provide them with a more comprehensive understanding of different aspects of the organization.

In particular, if your ultimate goal is to progress into a leadership position overseeing multiple departments, taking a step back can prove beneficial. It allows you to become more familiar with a department in which you may not have previously worked but may potentially lead in the future. By setting aside pride and being open to taking a step back, you can pave the way for multiple steps forward in your career trajectory.

While a step back may involve certain aspects that resemble a demotion, it can also offer valuable learning experiences and contribute to long-term professional growth. It is essential to maintain a broader perspective and prioritize personal development and future career prospects over immediate concerns about titles or compensation.

A Side Step

As a recruiter, I often advise candidates that a lateral move can be a favorable choice for their career development. Opting for a lateral move can present valuable opportunities for personal and professional growth while also aligning with their overall career strategy.

Here is an example of a lateral move within the HR field:

One of my colleagues was interested in exploring different areas of HR to determine his specialization. At the time, he held a coordinator position in talent acquisition. When an HR coordinator role became available, he decided to apply and accept the position. This lateral move enabled him to learn more about onboarding and gain valuable insights and expertise in that area.

It's crucial to evaluate individual skills, interests, and long-term career goals when determining the best career trajectory within HR. A lateral move can offer the chance to gain experience in different areas, broaden one's skill set, and eventually pave the way for advancement in the chosen specialization.

Let's look at the different career paths in HR and identify the best career trajectories for them.

Traditional

In the traditional HR career path, it is essential to cultivate a strong foundation of HR experience, knowledge, and leadership capabilities. Prioritizing opportunities to expand your HR knowledge becomes paramount. Once an individual feels confident in their HR skills, the next step is to pursue a role involving people management.

People management can take different forms within HR. One approach is through project management, where an HR professional takes on the responsibility of managing a specific project along with the team working on it. This allows them to exercise their leadership and organizational skills while collaborating with others to achieve project goals.

Another avenue for people management involves transitioning into a managerial position, overseeing a team within the HR department. This step requires not only expertise in HR but also the ability to lead, mentor, and guide a group of individuals towards shared objectives.

To progress along this career path, it is crucial to seek out opportunities that provide exposure to both HR-specific knowledge and people management experience. This might involve taking on challenging projects, pursuing additional training or certifications, and actively seeking leadership roles within HR teams or projects.

By combining HR expertise, continuous learning, and demonstrated leadership capabilities, professionals can advance within the HR field and enhance their overall career trajectory.

Specialty

Within the specialty career path in HR, the key focus is on honing expertise in a specific area of HR. This specialization entails concentrating on one particular aspect of HR and dedicating efforts towards developing specialized skills and knowledge in that area. Although the trajectory may involve progressing into leadership roles similar to the traditional career path, the distinction lies in the concentrated focus on a specific HR domain.

To pursue a specialty career path, it is crucial to identify the area of HR that aligns with your interests, strengths, and long-term career goals. Some examples of specialized HR areas include talent acquisition, employee relations, learning and development, compensation and benefits, HR analytics, diversity and inclusion, and HR technology.

Advancement within the specialty career path often involves progressing into leadership roles within the specialized area. This might include becoming a subject matter expert, a team lead, a manager, or even a director within that specialized HR function.

Specialty career paths offer the opportunity to become an expert in a specific HR area, allowing professionals to provide specialized insights, solutions, and value to their organizations. By focusing on skill development and pursuing leadership roles within their chosen specialty, HR professionals can thrive and excel in their careers while making a meaningful impact within their specialized HR domain.

Technical

In the HR technical career path, acquiring a deep understanding of various types of technology becomes crucial. Exploring opportunities within the Information Technology (IT) department can be an excellent strategy to gain the necessary technical experience.

Within HR, technology plays a significant role in areas such as HRIS (Human Resources Information Systems), data analytics, automation, and digital tools for recruitment and talent management. Therefore, developing technical proficiency is essential to effectively leverage technology in HR operations and initiatives.

By venturing into the IT department, HR professionals can gain exposure to different types of technology used in the organization. This exposure can provide valuable insights into the technical aspects of HR systems, databases, software applications, and IT infrastructure.

Working closely with IT professionals and collaborating on projects involving HR technology integration or enhancement allows HR professionals to enhance their technical competencies. They can learn about system configurations, data management, software implementation, and IT processes relevant to HR functions.

By pursuing the HR technical career path, HR professionals can become proficient in utilizing technology to streamline HR processes, analyze data for strategic decision-making, and enhance employee experiences. Their understanding of technology and collaboration with IT colleagues positions them as valuable contributors to driving digital transformation within HR and the broader organization.

Executive

If your ultimate career strategy involves reaching the C-Suite, developing strong business acumen is imperative. It's important to note that not all companies have a Chief Human Resources Officer (CHRO) position, particularly smaller organizations where roles such as Chief Operating Officer (COO), Chief Financial Officer (CFO), or Chief Administrative Officer (CAO) might have oversight over HR.

To position yourself as a strong candidate for executive roles in organizations without a dedicated CHRO, gaining experience in various areas of the business is highly beneficial. This broader perspective enables you to understand the interplay between HR and other functions, enhancing your ability to contribute strategically to organizational goals.

Consider seeking opportunities to work cross-functionally or take on projects outside of HR that expose you to different aspects of the business. This could involve collaborating with other departments, participating in interdepartmental initiatives, or volunteering for cross-functional teams. By doing so, you not only expand your knowledge but also demonstrate your ability to work effectively in a multidisciplinary environment.

By gaining experience and knowledge in diverse areas of the business, you become a stronger candidate for executive positions where a comprehensive understanding of the entire organization is valued. This demonstrates your capacity to align HR strategies with broader business objectives and make informed decisions that contribute to the overall success of the company.

When aiming for advancement within your company, it's crucial to decide on the specific route you want to pursue. Identify the desired role or position you aspire to and understand the skills, experience, and qualifications necessary for that position.

Once you have a clear target in mind, focus on making yourself the obvious choice for that role.

Chapter II

Obvious Choice

N ow that you know your next step toward your career strategy, you must develop yourself as the obvious choice for the role.

With workforce planning, companies will consider succession planning. Who will be the best person to take the role that is currently in the organization? Ideally, you want your name to be added to this conversation. How do you get your name included in succession planning conversations?

There was a time when I wanted my name in the succession planning conversation. My goal was to be the head of talent acquisition for the organization. I knew about the meetings and would ask questions about the meetings with my manager to gauge how I could be added to the list. Here is what I learned from my experience of becoming the obvious choice.

- Let it be heard: If you do not speak it, it will not happen. If you don't communicate your interest in the role, decision-makers may not be aware of your aspirations during the succession planning process. Make it a point to express your interest in the role to relevant individuals within the organization.

- Ask for advice and feedback. Assess your skills and experience to determine your readiness for the desired role. When expressing your interest to decision-makers, ask for their advice on how to build a compelling case for yourself. Additionally, request feedback on areas for improvement and what you can do to become a more effective leader. You can ask them the following questions to gain feedback.

What should I start doing, stop doing, or continue doing to be a more effective leader?

- Take the advice and feedback and go. Act upon the advice and feedback you receive, and follow up with the individuals who provided it. Demonstrate your willingness to learn and grow by implementing their suggestions. Schedule a follow-up meeting to discuss your progress and seek further guidance if needed.

- Raise your hand. Be proactive in seeking out projects or activities that can showcase your leadership, problem-solving, and decision-making skills. If you aim to transition to a different department, consider joining projects that involve collaboration with that department. By actively participating and contributing, you demonstrate your value as a team player and leader.

- Expand your network. Connect with individuals within the organization who can serve as mentors, advocates, or potential mentees. Cultivate relationships with these individuals over time, as strong connections can provide support and guidance throughout your career. Networking is an ongoing process that requires nurturing and maintaining.

- Be a top performer in your role. Continuously strive to be a top performer in your current position. Consistently meet and exceed expectations, and make a positive impact on the organization. Showcasing your skills and dedication in your current role increases the likelihood of being seen as an asset for future positions.

- Brand yourself as the obvious choice. Develop a personal brand that aligns with the qualities and attributes sought after in the desired role. Showcase your expertise through presentations, thought leadership, and active involvement in professional organizations or industry associations. Curate and share relevant content both internally and externally to establish yourself as a knowledgeable and credible professional.

- Speak up during meetings. Speaking up during meetings is a powerful way to showcase your expertise and stand out among your colleagues. When leaders or executives are present, sharing your thoughts and insights can demonstrate your value to the team and position you as an authority in your field. While it may feel daunting at first, speaking up can ultimately set you up for success by making your voice heard and contributing to meaningful discussions. So, don't hesitate to share your ideas and opinions during meetings – you never know the impact it could have on your career.

During my corporate career, I never hesitated to speak up during meetings, even in the presence of executives. I vividly recall a significant meeting where the CEO of the company was in attendance and posed a thought-provoking question: "What is keeping you up at night?" Surprisingly, there was silence; no one dared to respond. Feeling compelled to share, I spoke up and expressed my concerns. My contribution grabbed the CEO's attention, as it was a perspective that had not been raised before. This interaction made an impression, and when I later encountered the CEO at corporate headquarters, he remembered me and our previous conversation. It was evident that speaking up had made a lasting impact, one that might not have occurred if I had remained silent.

By following these steps, you position yourself as a standout candidate for the role, increasing your chances of being recognized as the obvious choice for advancement within your company. Stay committed to your goals, remain adaptable to changing circumstances, and continue seeking growth opportunities throughout your career journey.

A great time to discuss your career strategy and next steps in your career is during the performance review.

Chapter 12

Performance Review

A s a child, my dad gifted me with his knowledge about all sorts of things, like sports and my career. I remember in my 20s, he discussed how he handled performance reviews. He always gave himself the highest marks and provided lots of insights and data as to why he deserved them. Did he do this to gloat? No. My dad understood that his manager was a busy person who probably did not have enough time to write a thorough performance review, so he ensured that he provided all the information to make it easier for him/her. And guess what? It worked. His manager would agree to his high marks and his insights. A lot of times, his manager just copied and pasted what he wrote into the review. My dad taught me that I am my #1 cheerleader. You should be your #1 cheerleader in life, especially during the performance review. Your performance review gives you the ability to shine a light on your accomplishments and put a business case together for you to advance in the organization.

There have been several instances where the information I provided in my performance review was used by my manager. As a leader, I instilled the same practice in my team, encouraging them to compile relevant information for their reviews. To facilitate this process, it's crucial to maintain a comprehensive folder containing all pertinent information about your performance. This folder should include any commendations you've received, such as emails of appreciation or awards, along with past performance reviews, goals, and key performance indicators (KPIs). Keeping track of your progress towards these goals and KPIs, as well as documenting projects you've worked on, will ensure you have solid, well-rounded information to draw upon for your performance review. This proactive approach demonstrates your commitment to your role and can significantly impact the outcome of your review.

Now, not all managers will cut and paste your content for their performance review. But the more information you provide to them, the more reasons you deserve high marks on the review. It is key to a successful career to understand how to play the performance review game.

In life, we often encounter various games, and the performance review is no exception. Understanding this "game" and how to navigate it is crucial for achieving the highest ranking and merit increase possible.

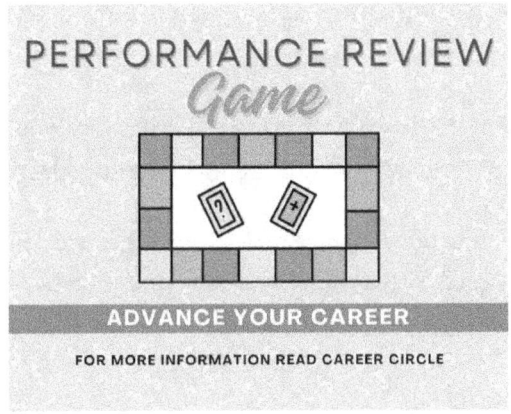

The Performance Review Game

2 players, Ages 18+

Objective: Your goal is to navigate through the performance review process and advance your career. Earn points by demonstrating your skills, achieving goals, and handling challenges effectively.

How to Play: Throughout the year, collect all your points and document your successes. Include key performance indicators, awards, accolades, and compliments from others. If your goal is advancement to management, include any projects or teamwork.

How to Win: Take all the information you've collected from the year and include it in the performance review form. Make sure it is easy to read and truly highlights you as the top performer. Always score yourself above average or above in rankings. Be prepared to include any areas you want to grow in and how you plan to develop those areas.

Bonus Points: Bring your career strategy to show your manager that you are serious about advancing in the organization.

Remember, the performance review process can feel like a game. Another lesson my dad taught me was that you always play the game...and you play to win.

Another big part of playing the career game is building strong relationships with co-workers, leaders, and stakeholders.

Chapter 13

Relationship Building

D id you know that having a best friend at work can increase your performance? A Gallup Study showed that employees with a best friend at work are more likely to engage customers and internal partners, get more done in less time, innovate, and share ideas while having fun at work.[15] Building relationships with others at your office can impact your ability to succeed in your career.

There are layers to relationships at work. Not everyone will be your BFF. These layers allow you to connect with more individuals, gain different perspectives, and obtain mentors and mentees to help with knowledge sharing.

Layers of Relationships:

Best Friend: Your go-to person who is your confidant and the person you will most likely continue a friendship with outside of work. Your BFF is a part of your tribe, the group of people who will always be there for you. BFFs are rare and do not always happen at each company. But when it does, you have a person who is on your team for life.

Work Friend: This is someone who you enjoy working with and get along well with. You may not go out after work together, but you definitely would have lunch with them. Ideally, you want work friends in your department plus in other areas of the business that you may support or work with occasionally.

Mentor: A mentor is someone you admire and respect, from whom you can learn and ask questions comfortably. While mentors typically hold higher roles, they can come from any area of the business. It's beneficial for your mentor not to be in the same department, as this provides more opportunities to learn about the business and share without potential reciprocal issues.

Go-To Person: A go-to person is someone who you know has the answers to questions that you have or information that you will need. This is someone you want on your team.

Mentee: Having a mentee gives you the ability to gift your knowledge and help someone with their career. Being a mentor takes time, energy, and effort. You need to be willing to step up and be the mentor you would want.

Use this graphic to identify a person who can fulfill each of these relationships for you at work.

Layers of Relationships

Best Friend · Work Friend · Mentor · Go-to Person · Mentee

How to Identify Key Relationships

Not everyone meets the qualifications to build a relationship at work. When considering individuals to build relationships with, look for shared interests, positive attitudes, and similar goals. Seek out colleagues who are reliable, respectful in communication, and compatible with your personality. Additionally, prioritize inclusivity by connecting with coworkers who value diversity. These factors can help you identify individuals with whom you can form meaningful friendships at work, contributing to a positive and supportive work environment.

Building the Relationship

Building relationships at work means understanding how interactions between people contribute to a positive and productive environment. The Golden Rule serves as a guiding principle, emphasizing the importance of treating others with respect, empathy, and fairness. This means being mindful of how your actions and words impact others and striving to create mutually beneficial relationships.

Authenticity plays a crucial role in building meaningful connections. By being genuine to yourself, you can foster trust and credibility with your colleagues. Authenticity also involves being transparent and honest in your interactions, which can help establish a foundation of respect and understanding.

In addition to authenticity, providing compliments and feedback can strengthen relationships. Recognizing and acknowledging the contributions of others can boost morale and create a supportive atmosphere. Similarly, offering constructive feedback shows that you care about the growth and development of your colleagues, fostering a culture of continuous improvement.

Moreover, being willing to apologize when necessary demonstrates humility and a willingness to take responsibility for your actions. Apologizing shows that you value your relationships and are committed to maintaining them, even when mistakes are made.

Overall, cultivating relationships at work is not just about networking or advancing your career; it's about creating a positive and fulfilling work environment for yourself and those around you. By following the Golden Rule, being authentic, and nurturing positive interactions, you can build strong and meaningful relationships that enhance your professional and personal life.

Part 4: Independence

I ndependence is when you are ready to go out on your own and have full ownership of your career strategy.

Chapter 14

Side Hustle

Starting a business can be an intimidating endeavor, and it may seem out of reach both in the present and in the future. There are undoubtedly risks, challenges, and an immense amount of hard work involved in building a successful business. However, embarking on this journey allows you to pursue your passions, attain independence, and potentially achieve financial prosperity. Additionally, starting a business offers personal growth, flexibility, and the chance to make a positive impact on both individuals and society as a whole. One effective way to test the waters and determine if entrepreneurship is right for you is by engaging in a side hustle.

My first venture into the world of side hustles was event planning, which I decided to brand as Acclaim Event Planning. The name "Acclaim" was chosen strategically as it would place my business at the forefront of the phone book's section, providing easy visibility and promotion. I worked on a diverse range of events, from fundraisers to family reunions, and it was a fulfilling experience to not only earn additional income but also engage my creative abilities. Unfortunately, due to personal reasons, I couldn't sustain this endeavor for long. Nevertheless, it provided me with a glimpse of the satisfaction and autonomy that comes with being your own boss.

When considering a side hustle, there are steps you can take to increase your chances of success. Here are some general steps to help you get started:

Identify your passion and skills: Think about your interests, hobbies, and skills that you can leverage to start a side business. Amy Clark who is an Executive Coach on the side of being a CHRO says that understanding what lights you up and gives you energy is crucial when balancing multiple roles.[16] Consider what you enjoy doing and what you're good at. This will help you choose a side hustle that aligns with your strengths and passions.

Here are a few HR side hustle ideas to consider:

- Resume Writing and Career Coaching: Use your HR knowledge to help individuals create effective resumes, cover letters, and LinkedIn profiles. Additionally, you can provide career coaching services, such as interview preparation, job search strategies, and career development advice.

- HR Training and Workshops: Conduct training sessions or workshops on HR-related topics, such as leadership development, employee engagement, diversity and inclusion, or conflict resolution. You can offer these sessions to companies or individuals looking to enhance their HR skills.

- <u>Freelance Recruiting:</u> Offer your recruitment skills and experience on a freelance basis. You can assist companies with sourcing and screening candidates, conducting interviews, and managing the hiring process.

- <u>HR Content Creation:</u> Start a blog, write articles, or create video content on HR-related topics. You can monetize your content through advertisements, sponsorships, or by offering premium content to subscribers.

Remember, before starting any side hustle, it's important to consider any legal and ethical considerations, such as potential conflicts of interest with your current employer, and ensuring you have the necessary expertise and qualifications to provide the services you offer.

Research the market: Once you have an idea, research the market to assess its viability. Look for competitors, target audience, and potential demand for your product or service. Identify any gaps or opportunities that you can tap into. While interviewing, David Shriner-Cahn, Founder of Smashing the Plateau, he stated that market research is crucial to understanding your potential customers and whether there is a need for your product or service. It helps you avoid investing time and resources into offerings that may not resonate with your target market.[17]

Define your target audience: Determine who your ideal customers or clients are. Understand their needs, preferences, and pain points. This will help you tailor your product or service to meet their specific requirements and improve your chances of success.

Develop a business plan: Create a roadmap for your side hustle by developing a business plan. Outline your goals, strategies, target market, pricing, marketing plans, and financial projections. A well-structured business plan will guide you throughout the process and serve as a reference point.

Here is a simple framework for a side hustle business plan:

- **Company Overview:** Provide an overview of your business, including the nature of the business, products/services offered, target market, and competitive advantage.

- **Value Proposition:** Clearly articulate the value you offer to customers.

- **Business Goals and Objectives:** Outline your goals for the first year, as well as for the next three and five years.

- **Product and Service Offering:** Provide details about your offerings, including features, benefits, and pricing.

- **Marketing and Sales Strategy:** Describe your marketing channels, pricing strategy, sales approach, and sales process.

- **Financial Projections:** Includes sales forecasts, budget, and initial investment or sources of financing.

- **Implementation Plan:** Create a timeline with tasks,

goals, and technology considerations.

Remember, your business plan doesn't have to be perfect, but it will help you understand what you need to do to make your side hustle successful.

Set clear goals: Establish both short-term and long-term goals for your side hustle. These goals should be specific, measurable, attainable, relevant, and time-bound (SMART). Setting goals will help you stay focused and motivated as you work towards building your business.

Determine your financial resources: Consider the financial resources you have available to invest in your side hustle. Determine your budget for things like product development, marketing, equipment, and any other expenses. It's essential to have a clear understanding of your financial situation and plan accordingly.

Create a legal structure: Decide on the legal structure for your side hustle. You may choose to operate as a sole proprietorship, partnership, limited liability company (LLC), or corporation. Consult with a legal professional or accountant to understand the legal and tax implications of each structure and choose the one that suits your needs.

When I started my event planning business, I operated as a sole proprietorship. When I ventured into my current businesses, I decided to establish limited liability companies (LLCs) for all of my businesses. Operating as an LLC provides me with certain legal and financial protections, as well as flexibility in managing and growing my ventures.

Register your business: Depending on your location and legal structure, you may need to register your side hustle with the appropriate government authorities. Obtain any necessary licenses or permits required to operate legally.

Registering a business with the state typically involves a cost of approximately $100. However, it's important to note that registration fees may vary depending on the state and the type of business entity you're establishing. It's recommended to check the specific requirements and fees in your state.

On the other hand, obtaining an Employer Identification Number (EIN) from the federal government is free of charge. An EIN is a unique identification number used by the Internal Revenue Service (IRS) to identify businesses for tax purposes. You can apply for an EIN online through the IRS website, and the process is straightforward and free of cost.

Remember to stay informed about any updates or changes in registration fees and procedures, as they may vary over time and in different jurisdictions. It's always best to consult with a legal professional or seek advice from the relevant government authorities to ensure compliance with the registration and tax requirements for your specific business.

Set up your operations: Establish the necessary infrastructure for your side hustle. This may include setting up a website, creating social media profiles, opening a separate bank account, and organizing your workspace or inventory. Consider the tools and systems you'll need to effectively run your business.

When selecting tools for your business, it's wise to consider free or low-cost options, especially when you're just starting. Here are some tools that I use in my business:

Free or Low Cost Business Tools

		Monthly Cost
Email & Drive	Google Work Place	Monthly Cost
Calendar Management	Google Calendar	Included in Workplace
Customer Relationship Management	Hubspot	Free & Paid Version
Accounting & Invoicing	Wave Apps	Free
Social Media Manager	Simplified	Free & Paid Version
Graphic Design/Website Creation	Canva	Free & Paid Version

Remember to explore other alternatives as well, as the tools mentioned above are just examples. Depending on your specific requirements, you may find different tools that align better with your business needs and budget.

Start marketing and selling: Develop a marketing strategy to promote your side hustle. Leverage digital platforms, social media, content marketing, and networking to reach your target audience. Begin selling your product or service and refine your marketing efforts based on customer feedback and market response. Bob Goodwin, President of Carer Club, recommends focusing on problem-solving in sales. Your product or service is the solution to a problem, and your job is to effectively communicate that.[18]

Referrals can be a powerful way to kickstart your side hustle. Don't hesitate to share your venture with your family, friends, and peers, as they can provide valuable support and connections. Your network can be an excellent source of potential clients or customers.

Remember, starting a side hustle requires time, effort, and dedication. It's essential to maintain a balance between your regular job and your side business while managing your energy and resources effectively.

If you decide to transition from a side hustle to full-time business owner, there are two primary options to consider: solopreneur and entrepreneur. The upcoming chapters will delve deeper into these options, providing more detailed information and guidance to help you make an informed decision about your entrepreneurial journey.

Chapter 15

Solopreneur

When I established my company in 2018, my idea of a successful business was shaped by certain assumptions. These notions revolved around having a team of employees, offering a wide range of services, and possibly operating from a physical location. These beliefs were influenced by my background, media portrayal, and various external factors. As I embarked on building my business, I envisioned a chance to expand by incorporating employees and transforming it into what I perceived as a 'real' business—a mini-RPO (Recruitment Process Outsourcing) company. The plan was to assist companies in their hiring processes by assembling a team of recruiters and leveraging technology. Encouraged by my business coach, who saw potential in this concept to build a seven-figure enterprise, I considered pursuing this path.

However, did I truly want to construct this business? No, I didn't. Did I believe it could pave the way for a successful venture? Yes, I did. Nevertheless, did I end up establishing this envisioned business? No, I did not.

It became apparent that my definition of a prosperous business needed reevaluation. I realized that managing employees, offering a multitude of services, or owning a physical establishment wasn't aligned with my true aspirations. Instead, I yearned for a business that I could nurture independently (with occasional support), take pride in, and provide for my family. Eventually, it dawned on me that becoming a Solopreneur was the ideal approach, and I came to recognize that being a Solopreneur can indeed lead to a successful business.

The definition of a solopreneur is:

> solopreneur (noun): one who organizes, manages, and assumes the risks of a business or enterprise without the help of a partner[19]

For me, a Solopreneur embodies the ability to operate a thriving business independently. As a Solopreneur, I hold the reins of decision-making within the business and can seek assistance whenever necessary. It's a one-person show where success is defined by the aspirations and efforts of the Solopreneur.

When discussing resumes and career search strategies with Nelly Grinfeld, we explored her journey and decision to become a solopreneur. Upon creating her company, Top of the Stack Resume, Nelly faced uncertainty regarding whether she would hire employees or subcontractors. However, she soon realized that her true passion lay in serving her clients directly, leading her to keep her business small and forgo managing employees.[20]

When considering a solopreneur business, you want to ensure that the type of business you are creating will work for a solopreneur. You want to leverage your skills, interests, and capacity to work independently. A few options that fit nicely as a solopreneur are consulting, coaching, freelancing in creative fields, content creation/blogging, professional services, and online courses.

While being a solopreneur might seem like you have to manage everything on your own, that's not the case! You don't have to tackle this journey alone. Building a network of skilled and knowledgeable individuals can significantly support your business, even if they are not traditional employees. "Networking can lead to collaboration opportunities. By connecting with other professionals in your industry or related fields, you may find opportunities to collaborate on projects, share resources, or co-create new offerings that benefit both parties", states David Shriner-Cahn.[21] These collaborations can not only enhance your business capabilities but also expand your reach and open up new possibilities for growth.

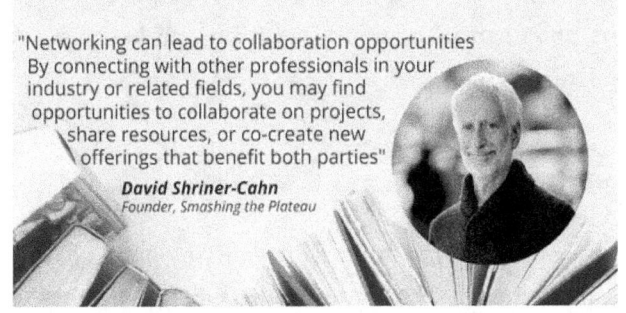

"Networking can lead to collaboration opportunities By connecting with other professionals in your industry or related fields, you may find opportunities to collaborate on projects, share resources, or co-create new offerings that benefit both parties"

David Shriner-Cahn
Founder, Smashing the Plateau

Consider assembling a tribe that encompasses the following roles:

Business Coach

A business coach can play a pivotal role in helping you establish a successful business that aligns with your vision. There are numerous reputable business coaches available. If budget is a concern, consider exploring free resources like SCORE, which provides mentorship to aid you and your business.

Virtual Assistant

Managing administrative tasks, scheduling, email correspondence, and customer support can be overwhelming. A virtual assistant can handle these tasks efficiently, giving you more time to focus on your business operations and serving your customers.

Accountant

Financial management may not be your strong suit. Hiring an accountant can alleviate the burden of managing books, tax preparations, and financial planning, ensuring your business's financial health.

Technology Expert

Embrace technology to streamline your solopreneurship journey. Automation and SEO optimization can significantly benefit your business. Engaging a technology expert ensures that your technological tools are optimized and functioning effectively.

Marketing Expert

Creating awareness and engagement with potential clients is essential. A marketing expert can assist in establishing your social media presence, crafting content marketing strategies, and executing digital marketing campaigns to reach your target audience effectively.

Public Relations Expert

Being recognized as an expert in your field through media exposure can significantly boost your business. Consider hiring a PR expert to assist with this.

Freelancers

There may be times when the workload exceeds your capacity. Hiring freelancers on a project basis can provide invaluable support during such busy periods, helping you meet client demands effectively.

Remember, while these individuals aren't your employees in the traditional sense, they form a vital support network that enables you to focus on what you do best while leveraging their expertise in various domains. Building a strong team of skilled professionals and resources can significantly contribute to the success and growth of your solopreneurial venture.

Transitioning from envisioning a traditional business model to embracing the concept of Solopreneurship has been a transformative journey. It has allowed me to focus on what truly matters to me: nurturing a business that I can be proud of, providing for my family, and enjoying the freedom and flexibility that comes with being independent. While the path of a Solopreneur may not be for everyone, it offers a unique opportunity to define success on your terms and build a business that aligns with your passions and aspirations. As I continue on this journey, I am excited about the possibilities that lie ahead and look forward to the growth and fulfillment that Solopreneurship has to offer.

If you are contemplating expanding your business to include employees, the upcoming chapter will offer valuable insights into the responsibilities and implications of becoming an employer. It will provide a comprehensive overview of the key considerations involved in hiring and managing employees, helping you make informed decisions as you grow your business.

Chapter 16

Entreprenuer

I s there a difference between a solopreneur and an entrepreneur? They can be the same, except when the entrepreneur wants to hire employees. This is where the two diverge. Deciding to hire a team is a significant step for any entrepreneur. There are key considerations to understand to make an informed decision on hiring employees. Let's explore those considerations.

First and foremost, assessing the financial health of the business is paramount. Can the business sustain employee salaries, benefits, and associated costs? Incorporating these expenses into the budget provides a comprehensive understanding of the overall costs of hiring employees. If you are unsure about the associated costs, a useful rule of thumb is to multiply the hourly rate by 1.25 to 1.4, factoring in taxes and benefit costs.

Equally important is grasping the legal obligations associated with hiring. Complying with labor laws, including minimum wage requirements, working hours, and employee rights, is essential. Familiarize yourself with tax obligations related to payroll and employee benefits. Consulting with an attorney to understand any legal obligations is recommended, keeping in mind that attorney fees are an additional cost to consider when hiring employees.

Once the financial and legal aspects are clear, the next step is to craft the role. Developing a detailed job description that outlines roles, responsibilities, desired experience, skills, and education is crucial. Consider establishing performance expectations, such as key metrics and goals, as well as details about the schedule, workplace, required resources, etc.

When deciding which roles to hire for first, consider the current needs of the business and what areas require assistance. Assessing where you need the most support and where you prefer to delegate responsibilities can help prioritize your hiring needs. Roles to consider include:

Operations Manager/Coordinator: Someone to oversee day-to-day operations, manage workflows, and ensure that takes are completed efficiently.

Sales and Marketing Specialist: Someone to help develop and implement sales and marketing strategies to attract and retain clients.

Assistant: Someone to handle administrative tasks, manage schedules, and provide support to the team.

Accountant: Someone to manage finances, handle payroll, track expenses and ensure compliance with tax laws.

Technical Support/IT: Someone to provide technical support, manage IT infrastructure and ensure smooth operation of systems.

Recruiting and hiring the right person for the role is the next step. While hiring friends or family who possess the required skill sets can be effective, it's crucial to assess whether they truly align with the skills needed. Implementing a targeted recruitment strategy to attract candidates with the right skill set is advisable if friends or family lack the necessary skills.

Establishing a systematic hiring process is key to ongoing success. This process should encompass various stages, from where the role is advertised to resume storage, the interview and offer process, and finally, onboarding. Developing a standardized hiring approach provides structure and consistency to your recruitment efforts, facilitating a smoother and more efficient hiring process in the future.

Additionally, focusing on onboarding and understanding how to effectively manage employees is essential. Developing an onboarding checklist alongside a training schedule can streamline the initial weeks for new hires. Implementing a regular cadence for one-on-one meetings, setting clear performance expectations, and establishing methods for tracking performance will contribute to a well-structured management approach.

There are several HR systems and technologies that can make the transition to becoming an employer seamless. Some key systems to consider include HR Information Systems (HRIS), Applicant

Tracking Systems (ATS), Payroll Systems, Time and Attendance Systems, and Performance Management Systems. When selecting HR technology, it's essential to choose systems designed for the size of your company to ensure cost-effectiveness. Additionally, some systems offer multiple HR functions in one, which can further reduce costs. Here are a few free or cost-effective HR technology companies to consider: Deel, Homebase, Connecteam, Bamboo, and Zoho People. For more information on HR technology, visit www.selectsoftwarereviews.com.

In conclusion, transitioning from a solopreneur to an entrepreneur who hires employees involves careful planning, financial assessment, legal compliance, and strategic recruitment. By understanding and addressing these key considerations, entrepreneurs can build a strong foundation for business growth and success.

Soloprenuer	Entreprenuer
✓ Works Alone	✓ Hires a Team
✓ Handles All Aspects of Business	✓ Delegates Tasks
✓ Hire Contractors	✓ People Manager

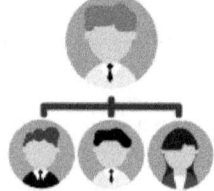

Chapter 17

Coaching vs. Consulting

When considering venturing out on your own in the field of Human Resources, two types of businesses that work well are HR Coaching and HR Consulting. Understanding the nuances of both can help you decide which path aligns best with your goals and aspirations.

HR Coaching primarily focuses on enhancing the skills, capabilities, and effectiveness of individual HR professionals or leaders within organizations. Coaches act as mentors, working closely with clients on a one-on-one basis or in small groups to identify goals, address challenges, and improve performance in specific areas of HR practice or leadership. Coaching engagements often revolve around personal and professional development topics such as leadership skills, communication, conflict resolution, career advancement, or specific HR competencies. The goal of HR coaching is typically to support the client in achieving personal or professional growth, enhancing their effectiveness in their current role, or preparing for future career opportunities.

On the other hand, HR Consulting involves providing strategic advice, solutions, and services to organizations to address broader HR challenges or initiatives. Consultants typically work with organizational leaders or HR departments to assess needs, diagnose issues, develop strategies, and implement solutions related to HR practices, processes, and systems. Consulting engagements may encompass a wide range of HR areas, including organizational design, talent management, workforce planning, performance management, employee engagement, compensation and benefits, HR technology, compliance, and change management. The goal of HR consulting is to help organizations improve their HR function, align HR strategies with business objectives, enhance organizational effectiveness, and achieve sustainable performance improvements.

The pricing models for both HR Coaching and HR Consulting can vary. Common approaches include hourly rates, package pricing (a set number of sessions or hours for a flat fee), retainers (fixed fee for access to a certain number of hours or services over a period), project-based pricing (a flat fee for specific HR projects or initiatives), outcome-based pricing (fee tied to the achievement of specific goals), and subscription-based models (ongoing monthly or annual fees for continuous access to services). Group sessions, where multiple clients participate in the same session, can offer a more cost-effective option. The choice of pricing model depends on the business model and the needs of the client.

In summary, HR coaching focuses on developing the skills and capabilities of individual HR professionals or leaders, whereas HR consulting involves providing strategic advice and solutions to organizations to address broader HR challenges and initiatives. Including both coaching and consulting services in your HR business can provide comprehensive guidance tailored to the unique challenges and opportunities in HR and your ideal clients.

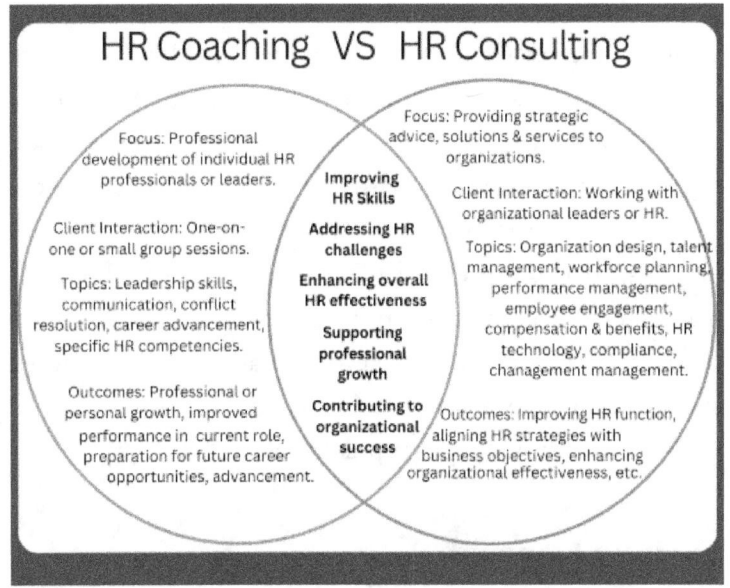

When deciding on the type of HR company you want to create, you can build your business from scratch or utilize a franchise. Both have pros and cons that should be carefully considered before making a decision.

Creating a Business from Scratch

Building a business from scratch refers to the process of creating a new company from the ground up, starting with an original idea or concept. This approach offers creative control over the business concept, branding, and operations, along with flexibility and unlimited potential. However, it comes with risks, limited support, and the need for significant time, effort, and investment to establish brand recognition and profitability.

When I decided to become an entrepreneur, I chose to create my business from scratch to make it truly my own. This decision required extensive research to understand how to build a business, market my services, and attract clients. I utilized a combination of free and paid resources to establish my business. Along the way, I experienced both successes and failures. Although I did not consider a franchise when starting out, looking back, I wish I had explored this option before deciding on the type of business to create. While I cannot say for certain that I would have chosen a franchise, I believe that understanding this business model would have enriched my entrepreneurial journey.

Buying a Franchise

Buying a franchise involves purchasing the rights to use an existing business name, branding, and business model. This option provides lower risk compared to starting from scratch, as the business model has already been tested and proven successful. Franchisees benefit from brand recognition, training, marketing support, and potentially easier access to financing. However, franchisees have less flexibility and autonomy compared to starting an independent business, as they must adhere to the franchisor's rules and guidelines, and success is tied to the overall success of the franchise.

When I think about a franchise, I think about brick-and-mortar stores or restaurants like McDonald's. However, there are several franchise options for consulting and coaching services.

Ultimately, the choice between creating a business from scratch and buying a franchise depends on your personal preferences, risk tolerance, and financial situation. Both options have the potential for success, but it's essential to carefully consider the pros and cons of each before making a decision.

Going out on your own in the world of HR can be a rewarding and fulfilling journey, but it requires careful planning, consideration, and a clear understanding of your goals and aspirations. Whether you choose to build your business from scratch or buy a franchise, the key is to align your business model with your passion and expertise to create a successful and sustainable HR business.

Before you commit to starting your own business, it's crucial to consider the following questions:

1. What is motivating me to start a business? Understanding your motivation will help you stay focused and committed when facing challenges.

2. What is my business idea, and is there a market need or demand for it? Conduct market research to validate your idea and ensure there is a viable market for your product

or service.

3. Should I pursue a franchise opportunity or build the company from scratch? Evaluate the pros and cons of each option based on your goals, resources, and preferences.

4. What resources do I have available to start and grow the business? Consider your financial resources, skills, network, and access to support.

5. Am I prepared to take on the risks and uncertainties associated with entrepreneurship? Be aware of the potential challenges and have a plan to mitigate risks.

6. How will starting a business impact my personal and professional life? Consider how starting a business will affect your time, finances, and relationships.

7. Am I ready to continuously learn and adapt to the changing business landscape? Entrepreneurship requires ongoing learning and adaptation to stay competitive.

By answering these questions, you'll gain a better understanding of your readiness to become an entrepreneur and embark on a new chapter in your HR career.

In summary, venturing into the world of entrepreneurship in Human Resources offers exciting opportunities for growth and impact. Whether you choose HR Coaching or HR Consulting, understanding the nuances of each and aligning them with your goals is key. Consider the pros and cons of starting from scratch versus buying a franchise, and evaluate your readiness by asking yourself key questions about motivation, market demand, resources, risks, and adaptability. By carefully considering these factors, you can embark on a rewarding entrepreneurial journey that aligns with your passion and expertise in the field of HR.

Conclusion

Wouldn't it be wonderful if there were a guide to help craft a well-defined career strategy, ensuring that each step brings me closer to my ultimate goal?

This question has been at the heart of my journey and is the driving force behind Career Circle. As we navigate the complexities of our careers, it's important to remember that clarity of purpose and a commitment to personal growth are key. By leveraging the insights and strategies outlined in this book, we can confidently pursue our career goals, build a strong foundation of expertise, and contribute to advancing the HR industry. Together, let's embrace the journey of growth and discovery, knowing that with the right guidance, we can achieve our ultimate career objectives and make a meaningful impact in Human Resources.

To further enhance your journey, consider using the Career Circle Workbook, a companion tool designed to complement the book. This workbook provides a structured framework for reflection, goal setting, and tracking your progress. By incorporating the workbook into your daily routine, you can deepen your understanding of the concepts presented in the book and accelerate your professional development. Here's to your continued growth and success in your HR career!

Thank you for taking this journey with me. I'm excited to see what is in store for you and your HR career. Cheers to a great life and career!

1. The Big Leap: Conquer Your Hidden Fear and Take Life to the Next Level, Gay Hendricks, 2009

2. https://www.truity.com/

3. https://www.123test.com/career-test/

4. https://www.mynextmove.org/explore/ip

5. https://hbr.org/2020/08/21-hr-jobs-of-the-future

6. https://hbr.org/2020/08/21-hr-jobs-of-the-future

7. https://www.aihr.com/t-shaped-hr-assessment/

8. Bob Goodwin, President of Career Club [Interview}. 22 August 2023

9. https://www.zippia.com/answers/what-percentage-of-hires-are-employee-referrals/

10. Nelly Grinfeld, Interviewee, Career Transition Expert, Top of the Stack Resume [Interview]. 5 October 2023.

11. Nelly Grinfeld, Interviewee, Career Transition Expert, Top of the Stack Resume [Interview]. 5 October 2023.

12. Peg Stookey, Executive Leadership Coach, Interview 28 September 2023.

13. Amy Clark, CHRO and Executive Coach [Interview]. 10 October 2023

14. Peg Stookey, Executive Leadership Coach, Interview 28 September 2023.

15. https://www.gallup.com/workplace/397058/increasing-importance-best-friend-work.aspx

16. Amy Clark, CHRO and Executive Coach [Interview]. 10 October 2023

17. David Shriner-Cahn, Founder of Smashing the Plateau [Interview]. 10 October 2023

18. Bob Goodwin, President of Career Club [Interview}. 22 August 2023

19. https://www.merriam-webster.com/dictionary/solopreneur

20. Nelly Grinfeld, Interviewee, Career Transition Expert, Top of the Stack Resume [Interview]. 5 October 2023.

21. David Shriner-Cahn, Founder of Smashing the Plateau [Interview]. 10 October 2023

Career Circle Workbook

C raft Your HR Career Strategy with the Career Circle Workbook. This comprehensive workbook provides templates and prompts designed to help you develop a strategic roadmap for your HR career. By utilizing these resources, you'll ensure that you have a solid game plan in place to navigate your professional journey in the field of Human Resources.

Acknowledgments

This is my third solo book, and with each book, I've been fortunate to have amazing people support me in so many ways. Thank you to my husband, *Ron*, for always supporting my crazy ideas. Thank you to my daughter, *Lena*, who has taught me so much about life and love. Thank you to my parents, *Larry and Becky Harmeyer*, for giving me the foundation to become the best version of myself. Thank you to my wonderful friend, *Jennifer Webber*, for editing and reviewing the book for me. Thank you to *Peg Stookey*, *Nelly Grinfeld*, *Amy Clark*, *Bob Goodwin*, and *David Shriner-Cahn* for sharing your wisdom. Thank you to all of my family, friends, and professional peers for supporting me through my entrepreneurial journey. I love you all!

About Author

Jodi Brandstetter, SHRM-SCP

Unique Brand Positioning Coach Best Selling Author Certified in Human Design & Design Thinking Speaker

Jodi is a seasoned Brand Positioning Expert specializing in human design and design thinking, dedicated to empowering HR business consultants who want to define their business based on their uniqueness. With two decades of business experience and certifications in design thinking and human design, Jodi stands out by offering tailored strategies that help HR consultants authentically connect with their ideal customers. As a HR Consultant herself, Jodi understands the challenges firsthand and has guided numerous clients to media recognition, collaborative publications, and business success through personalized approaches.

Jodi is an 8-time Amazon Bestselling Author who lives outside of Cincinnati, Ohio with her husband, daughter, and fur babies.

Contact Information:

LinkedIn: https://linkedin.com/in/jodibrandstetter

Website: https://jodibrandstetter.com

Also by Jodi Brandstetter

Hire By Design, A Hiring Blueprint with Design Thinking

HR By Design, Solving HR Challenges Through Design Thinking

Available on https://www.amazon.com/Jodi-Brandstetter/

www.ingramcontent.com/pod-product-compliance
Lightning Source LLC
Chambersburg PA
CBHW070424290526
45791CB00005B/1822

* 9 7 9 8 8 8 4 7 4 4 6 8 4 *